The Trial of Jeanne Catherine

The Trial of Jeanne Catherine

Infanticide in Early Modern Geneva

EDITED AND TRANSLATED BY SARA BEAM

UNIVERSITY OF TORONTO PRESS
Toronto Buffalo London

© University of Toronto Press 2021
Toronto Buffalo London
utorontopress.com

Printed and bound by CPI Group (UK) Ltd, Croydon, CR0 4YY

ISBN 978-1-4875-8768-0 (cloth)   ISBN 978-1-4875-8769-7 (EPUB)
ISBN 978-1-4875-8767-3 (paper)   ISBN 978-1-4875-8770-3 (PDF)

Library and Archives Canada Cataloguing in Publication

Title: The trial of Jeanne Catherine: Infanticide in early modern Geneva / edited and translated by Sara Beam.
Names: Beam, Sara, editor, translator.
Description: This volume presents all the documents of the trial, translated into English from the original French. | Includes bibliographical references and index.
Identifiers: Canadiana (print) 2020034403X | Canadiana (ebook) 20200344188 | ISBN 9781487587680 (cloth) | ISBN 9781487587673 (paper) | ISBN 9781487587697 (EPUB) | ISBN 9781487587703 (PDF)
Subjects: LCSH: Thomasset, Jeanne Catherine – Trials, litigation, etc. – Sources. | LCSH: Trials (Infanticide) – Switzerland – Geneva – History – 17th century – Sources. | LCSH: Infanticide – Switzerland – Geneva – History – 17th century – Sources. | LCSH: Criminal justice, Administration of – Switzerland – Geneva – History – 17th century – Sources. | LCSH: Motherhood – Switzerland – Geneva – History – 17th century – Sources. |
Classification: LCC KKW172.I54 T75 2021 | DDC 345/.49451602523–dc23

We welcome comments and suggestions regarding any aspect of our publications – please feel free to contact us at news@utorontopress.com or visit us at utorontopress.com.

University of Toronto Press acknowledges the financial assistance to its publishing program of the Canada Council for the Arts and the Ontario Arts Council, an agency of the Government of Ontario.

 Canada Council   Conseil des Arts
for the Arts   du Canada

ONTARIO ARTS COUNCIL
CONSEIL DES ARTS DE L'ONTARIO
an Ontario government agency
un organisme du gouvernement de l'Ontario

Funded by the   Financé par le
Government   gouvernement
of Canada   du Canada

 Canadä

Contents

Illustrations

Acknowledgments

This book owes its genesis to Phil and Judy Benedict, who generously hosted me in their Geneva home while I conducted many research trips to the archives. On one of those trips, I discovered the trial of Jeanne Catherine and realized that her story needed to be told. Generous support from the Office of Research Services at the University of Victoria and a fellowship at the Centre for Studies in Religion and Society enabled me to do so. This project is very much indebted to the efficient professionalism of the staff at the Genevan state archives who made it possible to access precious resources in a timely fashion. I relied heavily on the help of doctoral student Justine Semmens in the early stages of the translation and on the expert advice of literary scholar Claire Carlin in its final stages. The willingness of my "virtual convent" colleagues Megan Armstrong, Penny Roberts, and Virginia Reinburg to read an early draft was invaluable as always. Thanks also go to my daughter Iris Fairley-Beam who read the trial with the critical eye of a student and so helped to make this edition more accessible and engaging.

Introduction

I. HISTORICAL BACKGROUND

On May 6, 1686, in the small village of Laconnex outside of Geneva, two children suddenly died: a two-year-old girl named Jeanne and a five-year-old boy whose name we will never know. They both fell ill that morning, first nauseous and lethargic, then vomiting, drooling, having convulsions. Neighbors were called in to help and various remedies were applied. Over the course of the morning their suffering continued to intensify. They died that afternoon, within a few minutes of one another, in the presence of a local apothecary, who suspected poisoning. The boy's distressed parents, a farm laborer named Abraham Clerc and his wife, latched onto this explanation. Poisoning. Who was to blame?

They did not have to look far. That morning they had received an unexpected visit from the mother of little Jeanne, a noblewoman from the lands northeast of Geneva herself named Jeanne Catherine Thomasset. Two years earlier, this foreign noblewoman had given birth to her illegitimate daughter in the village of Laconnex and had left her in the care of Abraham Clerc's wife. Jeanne Catherine had visited her daughter on a number of occasions, but on May 6th she was accompanied by an unknown middle-aged man, her cousin Daniel de la Fléchère. Soon after they arrived, the children fell ill. Sometime later in the morning, at a moment when the children seemed to be sleeping, Jeanne Catherine and Daniel left and walked back to Geneva. To the inhabitants of Laconnex, who claimed both children had been healthy and running around the village the day before, the visit of the strangers clearly precipitated their deaths.

As a result, Abraham Clerc, father of the dead boy, left for Geneva, determined to denounce Jeanne Catherine as a murderer. He found her wandering the city streets, distressed; she had already heard a rumor that the children might have died. Jeanne Catherine urged Abraham to return with her to Laconnex to tend to the children. She seemed confused and had not fully accepted that the children were dead. Instead, Abraham insisted that they go together to report the deaths to a city official. By that night,

Jeanne Catherine was arrested and in prison, accused of poisoning the two children.

A foreign world of noblemen and peasants, wet nurses, unfamiliar remedies, and sudden death. A puzzle: why had the children died and why was it so obvious that someone needed to be blamed? The deaths of these two children led to a criminal trial complete with rich witness testimony, reports by medical experts, many interrogations of Jeanne Catherine (some with torture), personal letters sent by her family to the Genevan criminal court, and correspondence between Genevan officials and officials in nearby Switzerland where Jeanne Catherine's family lived. For a few months in 1686, the city of Geneva was riveted by the trial of Jeanne Catherine. This volume presents all the documents of the trial, translated into English from the original French, telling the fate of the children and of the accused murderer Jeanne Catherine.

Criminal trial documents from the early modern world are precious records of lived experience, traces of people that we have otherwise lost. Many of the voices we hear in these records are the voices of people who could not write or were unlikely to do so, most notably those of peasants and women, even elite women like Jeanne Catherine. Yet the trial record does not provide a transparent window into their lives. By definition, criminal prosecutions investigate potentially illegal behavior and the people summoned to court to testify are either trying to condemn the suspect or defend their innocence. As a result, trial records capture conflicting stories of what happened and why it happened, each story designed to represent the person telling their version as positively as possible.

This is certainly true for everyone involved in the trial presented here. The peasants of Laconnex asserted the children had been entirely healthy before Jeanne Catherine arrived on May 6th, even though both Jeanne Catherine and the wet nurse agreed that at the very least they were suffering from intestinal parasites. In doing so, the villagers not only sought to blame Jeanne Catherine but also to protect themselves from any counter-accusation that they were somehow responsible for the children's deaths. Jeanne Catherine, from the first and throughout the trial, denied having killed the children and claimed to have been an attentive mother to her daughter. She clearly hoped to save her own life and vindicate herself before God. Other witnesses, such as the physicians who submitted a formal report after autopsying the children, were also telling a story: by describing in detail the chemical experiments they undertook to determine whether poison had been administered, the physicians were asserting that they were men of science, certified professionals whose testimony should be believed. Even the court clerks, by laboriously collecting all the

testimony, recording it, and organizing it to be preserved for future generations, told a story of having followed the legal procedures to the letter in
ways that justified the final sentence. When reading the trial, we need to be
attentive to all of these stories, notice where they come together and where
they diverge. We can find meaning in the stories told and the stories left
untold and somewhere in the mix try to figure out what happened.

But we should also remember that we have been given only a partial
account of Jeanne Catherine's trial. Partial because we know documents
were left out for one reason or another: officers confiscated several personal letters from Jeanne Catherine's bedchamber, but only two of them
are available to us; some letters exchanged between the Genevan criminal
court and officials in Nyon and Bern are not included in the trial record;
Jeanne Catherine's family tried to slip notes to her in prison, and likely suc-
ceeded in doing so, but we will never see them.

We will also never be able to fully reconstruct her trial because we cannot be there in the flesh. We did not see the body language of Abraham
Clerc and Jeanne Catherine Thomasset when they first came before the
court investigator the evening of May 6th. Did Jeanne look afraid? Did
she cry? Did she fall on her knees when she declared her innocence? Did
the pain of having lost his son show on the face of Abraham and move
the investigator, a father himself, to take up the case? We know that early
modern judges were attentive to non-verbal signs of guilt, innocence,
penitence, stubborn determination. We know that bodily signs such as
pallor or tremors informed their judgments. Sometimes these signs were
recorded in the documents, just often enough for us to understand how
important they could be, but not regularly enough for us to be able to read
the courtroom dynamics, even if we could be sure to interpret the gestures
correctly.

For we cannot assume that Jeanne Catherine or any of the many individuals involved in this trial moved, felt, or thought of their place in their
family, in their community, or before God in the same way that we would.
People who study communities different from their own, whether distin-
guished by time, by place, or by other markers such as race/ethnicity or
class, have long since understood that a person's sense of themselves is
specific to their lived experience, which in turn is profoundly shaped by
the stories told to them throughout their lives to make sense of the world.
Our dynamic understanding of who we are and how our lives are mean-
ingful are expressed through stories, told to us and told by us to friends/
family, to employers/judges, to sacred persons/places, to ourselves. How
individuals in Jeanne Catherine's world understood themselves as good or
bad people and the scripts to which they tried to fit their experience need to

be investigated and not assumed. Jeanne Catherine's trial occurred almost three hundred and fifty years ago. This introduction provides some information about gender, family, place, religion, and the judicial system that will make her trial easier to interpret.

Finally, the full truth of any historical trial is elusive because the past is gone. What happened *did* happen, but its reality was fleeting and cannot be brought back to life. All we have are these fragments, bits of paper in sometimes difficult-to-read handwriting, a mere shadow of what occurred. But these shadows are rich and suggestive. Reading a criminal trial is an act of discovery as the reader tries to fit the pieces of the puzzle together. The pieces of Jeanne Catherine's trial need to be examined carefully, compared one with the other, and assessed for what they have to offer.

a. Jeanne Catherine Thomasset

Jeanne Catherine was born into a minor French-speaking noble family based in nearby Switzerland, the second daughter of Jean François Thomasset and his wife Louise de Brétigny. All told, the Thomasset couple had at least nine children, eight of whom survived until adulthood, which would have been exceptional at a time when child mortality was high. Records indicate that Jeanne Catherine was baptized on May 6, 1654, which means that she was about thirty-two years old at the time of the trial even though she claimed that she was only twenty-six. Jeanne Catherine likely spent most of her youth living in the village of Agiez, where her father was the hereditary mayor and owned a manor house. She regularly visited the small city of Orbe, where her father enjoyed *bourgeois* status, and lived for periods of time with various relatives throughout the Vaud region northeast of Geneva.

The Thomassets were a well-established noble family based in the Vaud region of Switzerland, the lands between the north shores of Lake Geneva and Lake Neuchatel. The Thomassets were rich in land and served as tax assessors for Bern, the Swiss city that ruled over the Vaud. The family had enjoyed noble status since the fifteenth century, but they were not among the highest-ranking nobles in the region. These were the noble families of Lausanne and Bern and the leading military noble families who served Bern as bailiffs of the different districts (*bailliages*) of the Vaud. The Thomassets had instead become noble through their service as notaries and their gradual purchase of large numbers of seigneuries, fiefs that allowed them to exact labor and dues from local peasants. In addition to marrying into other noble families, the Thomassets forged marriage bonds with *bourgeois* families in Orbe and also with families that lived in Genevan territory. The Régis brothers of Geneva, who arranged to pay the wet nurse on Jeanne

Catherine's behalf, were cousins. Possibly Monsieur de Chasteauvieux of Cologny, who allowed Jeanne Catherine to stay at his home briefly late in her pregnancy, was also tied by marriage or alliance to the Thomasset family. Jeanne Catherine's family thus cast a wide net over a large region, and some members of that network were willing to help a wayward young woman seeking a safe but discreet place to give birth. The Thomassets were well enough connected that they could even draw on the support of the highest echelons of the Vaud nobility, including Nicolas Steiguer, bailiff of Nyon, and Romier Laisné, another prominent relative, to support them in their effort to influence the outcome of Jeanne Catherine's trial.

Jeanne Catherine would have been accustomed to living in a large household comprised of relatives, servants, stable hands, and tutors. Peasants seeking work and aiming to resolve local conflicts would have turned to Jeanne Catherine's father at the modest château in Agiez. Jeanne Catherine would have been educated at home alongside her siblings. She clearly was very comfortable writing letters to relatives. We know she was very close to at least one of her siblings, her brother Samuel: they exchanged affectionate letters and even shared a lodging in Geneva together after the birth of her illegitimate daughter. As a result, Jeanne Catherine's upbringing, wealth, and educational level would have placed her at a great distance from the peasants with whom she was interacting in Laconnex. Her social confidence and even arrogance sometimes come through in the documents.

Jeanne Catherine lived in a profoundly patriarchal society in which men held positions of power and owned almost all property. In early modern Europe, females were seen as equal to males in the eyes of God but otherwise lesser than the more perfect version of humanity: men. As a daughter, Jeanne Catherine would have been expected to obey her parents, become a good Christian, and marry a man who would bring additional connections, land, and/or wealth into the family. While noble families in this period did sometimes take the personal inclinations of their children into account when selecting a marriage partner, everyone understood that marriage choice was primarily a question of forging family alliances and securing status and wealth. Until a young woman married, fathers remained legally responsible for their daughters. Once married, a noblewoman became the legal responsibility of her husband, but in some situations she might still be able to exercise some control over her dowry, the money or lands her family gave to her husband before the wedding. Jeanne Catherine may have shared her family's hopes that she would marry well and further the family line.

Noble families like the Thomassets normally married their daughters off in their late teens to their early twenties. In 1668, when Jeanne Catherine's older sister Marthe was seventeen years old, she married Jacob

François Margel, a Protestant pastor whose career took him to various parishes in the Vaud. We do not know the size of her sister's dowry, but it was unlikely to have been large. Her marriage to a minister indicates that the family was pious, but, from a social standpoint, the alliance was less lucrative than marriages among noble families that earlier generations of Thomassets had secured. Ministers were generally well educated, but did not enjoy noble status and did not earn a large income from their pastoral work. This choice of marriage partner for Marthe may have reflected the family's financial vulnerability and the fact that Jeanne Catherine's father had four adult daughters to marry off, an expensive proposition. By the 1680s, we know that Jeanne Catherine's father had amassed a significant level of debt, and he began to sell off or mortgage family lands to repay it. It is very probable that he could not afford to dower any of his daughters at a high enough rate to attract a noble husband. The fact that Jeanne Catherine was still unmarried as she approached her thirtieth birthday is notable and suggests that the family accepted that she would remain single all her life, a social and financial burden on the family.

In 1683, Jeanne Catherine had sex with a man and became pregnant. The Genevan court at first suspected that the father of her child was her cousin Daniel de la Fléchère, a married man, but she emphatically denied this. Authorities later accused Jonas Roch of Orbe, also a cousin of Jeanne Catherine's, of being the father of her child. Although she initially claimed not to know the name of her sexual partner, she eventually admitted that Jonas was responsible. We do not know how secretive the relationship between Jeanne Catherine and Jonas might have been: possibly it was a brief clandestine affair, but just as likely the relationship was known to and informally approved by her family, who would have considered the Roch family, a *bourgeois* family of lawyers, to be a respectable connection. On the other hand, it is also possible that Jonas was too closely related to Jeanne Catherine for the marriage to be deemed acceptable by the church.

Jeanne Catherine testified to the Genevan authorities that her parents did not know about her sexual relations with Jonas and the birth of her illegitimate daughter. Evidence gleaned from her personal letters, however, clearly shows that her daughter was an open secret within the family. It was after all not uncommon, even among the nobility, for young couples to have sex once they intended to marry. So, if we assume Jeanne Catherine and Jonas were informally betrothed, their behavior would not have been out of the ordinary, even though it was frowned upon by the Protestant church. Once Jeanne Catherine became pregnant, her family would have expected Jonas to marry her. His family seems to have resisted the marriage, possibly because the dowry offered was insufficient. But it seems that someone in the Roch family promised to pay for the upkeep of her illegitimate child. The Roch family might have hoped that the baby, sent out to a wet nurse, would quietly die, as many infants did in the seventeenth century.

Because the Thomassets were subjects of the Swiss city of Bern, when rumors began to circulate that Jeanne Catherine had given birth to a child out of wedlock, a local minister reported her crime to the church court in Bern and to the local bailiff of Romainmôtier, the Vaud district in which Agiez was located. Had she been caught, the authorities in Bern might have required a formal apology from Jeanne Catherine, issued her a fine, prevented her from participating in church rites until she repented, and possibly even sent her briefly to prison. Judging from a letter that her brother Samuel wrote to her, Jeanne Catherine's father may have tried to defend her honor with the authorities. It is likely that Jeanne Catherine was living in Geneva, a separate republic adjacent to the Vaud, in order to avoid criminal prosecution in Bern. Even though her family clearly knew Jeanne Catherine had had a baby, it did not welcome the shame that would have resulted from the public exposure of Jeanne Catherine's sexual license and failure to marry.

As noble landowners, the Thomassets would have been accustomed to being at the pinnacle of the local circles in Agiez and they would have demanded to be treated with the honor befitting their status. Maintaining male honor for members of the nobility involved offering protection to their clients and allies, managing their financial affairs responsibly, being willing to take up arms as needed, and serving their patrons and rulers, in this case the Bernese, well. Family honor also hinged on the good behavior of the Thomasset women: women were expected to defer in public to their menfolk and to remain sexually chaste (virgins before marriage and monogamous afterward). If the family honor was compromised or respect or deference were not forthcoming, it was not uncommon for nobles to lash out physically at the offending party, sometimes causing injury to their opponents' good reputation but also often inflicting physical wounds that could, in an age before antibiotics, lead to accidental death. In nearby France, nobles regularly appealed to the king of France to pardon them when they accidentally killed fellow nobles who had insulted their honor; the attackers usually received a pardon, which meant they were not prosecuted for having committed these "accidental" homicides. If the person who insulted a nobleman was of inferior rank, violence against them was even more justified. Not to defend one's honor was to lose face not only for oneself but for one's entire family. Honor conflicts between noble families could sometimes last for generations, involve multiple violent conflicts, and establish longstanding vendettas between families. It is clear from

View of seventeenth-century Geneva

CH Archives d'État de Genève (AEG) Archives privées 247/1/22.

personal letters included in the trial that the Thomassets saw the world as clear-cut, divided into allies and enemies, and that family honor was an important commodity in their world.

It is in this context that we need to understand the Thomasset family's interventions in Jeanne Catherine's trial. Her father, together with a number of male relatives, wrote repeatedly to Geneva demanding her immediate release. Even though these letters acknowledged that Geneva was an independent republic possessing the authority to judge criminal matters as it saw fit, the assertive tone of these letters indicates that the Thomassets considered the judges of the Genevan criminal court to be their social inferiors who ought to heed their requests.

b. The Protestant republic of Geneva

Whereas Jeanne Catherine was a subject of Bern, she was accused of having poisoned the two children within the territory controlled by the independent republic of Geneva, which, at the time, was not part of Switzerland. The city of Geneva had been ruled indirectly by the Duke of Savoy during the medieval period, but more recently Geneva proclaimed its independence. After 1536, the city recognized no higher political authority and all political, executive, and judicial powers were administered by elected councils of men drawn from the upper echelons of Genevan society. The most important council, which had considerable executive power over daily affairs, diplomatic missions, and judged criminal matters, was the Small Council, a group of twenty-five elite men nominally elected annually but, in reality, re-elected year after year for decades. These councillors, all of them citizens of Geneva, were large-scale landowners and long-distance merchants. The Small Council was led by four executive officers chosen among the councillors called syndics. One of them, known as the first syndic, functioned as the mayor of the city. In 1686, the first syndic was Pierre Fabri, a seventy-year-old citizen, landowner, and member of an ancient, well-respected Genevan elite family. The honor of being elected to the Small Council granted these men the title of "noble" regardless of whether they owned extensive lands near the city. A minority of them had formal legal training, but this was not required to serve on the council. Together, as a group, these elite Genevan men would decide Jeanne Catherine's fate.

Geneva in 1686 was a small republic consisting of a city of some 16,000 inhabitants whose territory stretched at most only a few kilometers from the city walls. Geneva was mostly surrounded by lands controlled by the Catholic dukes of Savoy, though a small corridor of land along the north side of Lake Geneva directly bordered the Vaud region ruled by its most important Protestant ally, the Swiss city of Bern. Although the Genevan government regularly consulted with Bern and other Swiss Protestant cities on political, diplomatic, and judicial matters, the city was fiercely proud of its autonomy and resented all encroachments on its fragile independence. As a tiny polity on the edge of the Swiss confederation, Geneva was always dependent for its very survival on diplomatic alliances and the inclinations of its neighbors. This dependence on good relations with its neighbors was reflected in Jeanne Catherine's trial. Because she was a subject of Bern and not of Geneva, the Small Council wrote to the authorities there requesting permission to prosecute her. The Bernese quickly wrote back that they could do as they pleased with Jeanne Catherine: they were certainly not going to come to her rescue, probably because she was already considered to be a fugitive.

A prosperous late medieval city known for its long-distance fairs, Geneva had been renowned since the sixteenth century for its religious leadership in the international Protestant movement. Protestantism as we know it was inadvertently initiated by Martin Luther, a Saxon monk concerned about corruption in the Catholic church who was, as a result, expelled from that church in 1520 and then helped to establish a new church in "protest." Over the next few decades, Protestant communities sprang up throughout northern Europe and some states followed Saxony in abandoning the Catholic church. In Geneva, a group of powerful Protestant converts led the city to break with the Catholic church in the 1530s, the same decade that the city established its independence from the House of Savoy. A few years later, in 1541, John Calvin, a French Protestant, was invited to take up the leadership of this fledgling church. He forged a new form of Protestantism, known variously as Reformed, Calvinist, or Presbyterian, that eventually spread to France, the Netherlands, Hungary, Germany, England, and Scotland. After the establishment of the Reformation, the social and economic makeup of early modern Geneva was increasingly dependent on waves of religious exiles, mostly Protestant converts fleeing discrimination in predominantly Catholic France. These refugees arrived in a first wave in the mid-sixteenth century. More recently, a change in royal policy that outlawed Protestantism in France in 1685 resulted in a second wave of religious exiles seeking refuge in Geneva. These refugees brought financial capital, high levels of education, and skills to the city, but also put significant pressure on the urban infrastructure.

The social structure of Geneva was similar to many Swiss and German cities. A small elite of citizens and prosperous *bourgeois* ran city affairs, but the bulk of residents held little political power and were less economically secure. Down one rung from the urban elite were the professionals: physicians, professors at the local Protestant seminary, trained lawyers, and

Protestant ministers. These families possessed prestige from their levels of education but were less wealthy than the landholding and merchant elites. The large group of artisans who plied trades from butcher, baker, and master surgeon to silk cloth manufacturer were still, for the most part, financially secure. These families often owned a house in the city and ran their businesses out of their home, with the front room of the ground floor serving as a shop to sell their wares. Some men of the artisan class were also sharecropping farmers who farmed an elite family's land for a share of the profits. Some artisan families rented rooms in their houses to workers. By far the largest group living in the city, making up a majority of city residents, was the working poor: the men were day laborers and staffed the local militia; the women worked in the textile trades, sold retail goods in the market, as well as working as wet nurses and servants.

Despite these social and economic disparities, Geneva was a small and intimate community. Early modern Geneva was a compact urban area, surrounded by walls, located at the southwest tip of Lake Geneva as it emptied into the powerful Rhone River. The entire area contained within the city walls could be crossed on foot in less than fifteen minutes. Most of the community was located on the south side of the lake on a floodplain. The Genevan city hall, where criminals were judged, was located at the top of a hill overlooking this floodplain, a site that the Romans had settled centuries earlier. St. Pierre Cathedral, which rang out the hours of the day and was the largest church in town, faced the lake some way up that same hill. Jeanne Catherine rented a room from a well-established widow right around the corner from the cathedral and the city hall, located in one of the four- and five-story stone houses that lined the Place Bourg-de-Four, an open square near the top of the same hill. From her home, Jeanne Catherine could walk to the city ramparts on the Boulevard Saint-Antoine in a minute or two. Had she chosen to do so, she could have slipped out of Genevan territory the afternoon the children died without much notice, though a noblewoman traveling alone would always have been a subject of interest.

Living in close quarters, cheek by jowl, in crowded buildings where families slept several people to a room and most sociability occurred in kitchens that spilled out onto the street or a courtyard, it was difficult for much to remain secret for long in Geneva. Neighbors knew each other by name, knew whose marriages were troubled because they could hear the shouting, knew which children refused to do their chores, which journeymen working for local artisans came home late after a night of drinking. People living in the Place Bourg-de-Four would have known that the widow Fabri was renting a room to a young noblewoman from the Vaud, who spoke with an accent perhaps, and was rumored to have had an illegitimate child. Jeanne Catherine denied having ever told her landlady that she had a daughter in Laconnex: this is very probable, but it is also clear that the widow Fabri knew perfectly well why Jeanne Catherine was living alone, far from her family, out of reach of the law in Bern. The peasant women of Laconnex who testified against Jeanne Catherine claimed not to know her name, only that she was a "foreigner." But Abraham Clerc, who regularly received payments on his wife's behalf for her wet-nursing services, knew exactly where to find Jeanne Catherine when he came to Geneva to accuse her of murder. When they ran into each other near her home, Jeanne Catherine urged Abraham and his uncle to keep their voices down and to come up to her bedchamber where they could talk further because she feared that passersby would overhear their conversation. But Abraham refused: he proclaimed his accusation against her, that she had poisoned his son, loudly and clearly for everyone to hear. Rumors were already flying that Jeanne Catherine was a murderer; the community would have been shocked to hear that this aloof stranger had poisoned two children, one of them her own flesh and blood.

Late seventeenth-century Geneva was a profoundly Protestant place. Even so, most Genevans were far from perfect Christians, and they might be quick to judge a foreigner whose relative wealth they might envy and lifestyle they might gossip about to friends and neighbors. Like other Christian denominations, the Reformed Protestant church upheld the central doctrine of Christianity, that the sacrifice of Jesus Christ, son of God, when he was crucified by the Romans, allowed for the possibility of eternal salvation for all faithful Christians. But the day-to-day experience of living as a Christian in Geneva was distinct from nearby Catholic experiences. The Protestant church abolished the Catholic Mass, with its incense and promises of a miracle every time the priest consecrated the bread and wine, replacing it with long sermons and the occasional Protestant communion. The state removed sacred images and statues from the churches, banned the worship of most saints, and outlawed dancing, gambling, and most popular festivals. For a time, at the outset of the Reformation, the new Protestant church even tried to abolish Christmas, which it saw as a pagan celebration, though it was not able to do so for long: the people insisted on retaining this popular festival. Protestant church leaders aimed to establish a pure church true to the original intentions of Christ and to forge a new disciplined Christian community in which all residents followed the strictures of the new church, including more stringent punishments for those who enjoyed extramarital sex. By the 1680s, most Genevans identified with

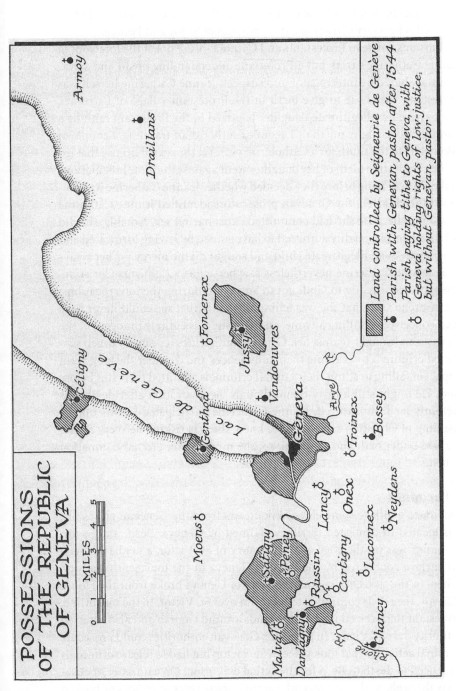

Map of Geneva and surroundings
Calvin's Geneva, John Wiley and Sons.

this Protestant faith and saw Geneva as a righteous island surrounded on most sides by lesser Christians, the Catholics of Savoy and France.

Tensions between Protestants and Catholics were not at the forefront of Jeanne Catherine's trial, but a Protestant understanding of sin and salvation was shared by interrogator and suspect. Jeanne Catherine herself was Protestant; she chose to give birth in the Protestant village of Laconnex and to have her illegitimate daughter baptized in the Protestant faith by a minister in Cartigny north of Laconnex rather than traveling a couple of kilometers to the south for a Catholic service. Yet the sexual license that led to the clandestine birth of her daughter went against the moral regulations of the church. Long before they decided whether Jeanne Catherine had poisoned the children, the Genevan prosecutors identified Jeanne Catherine as a sinner because she had committed extramarital sex. Notably, she did not disagree. She readily admitted to have sinned by having fornicated and given birth to an illegitimate child and sought divine mercy for her weakness. Jeanne Catherine nevertheless saw herself as a righteous Christian. She appealed directly to God, not to any saint, during the interrogations. She swore to God that she was telling the truth, that she could never have even conceived of killing anyone, and that she was entirely innocent of the accusations brought against her. Genevan authorities repeatedly urged suspected criminals to examine their consciences and consider the long-term impact of failing to admit their guilt. If criminals admitted their sins before God, He might still forgive them, though their salvation after death was certainly far from assured. Jeanne Catherine participated in this understanding of Christian salvation: she knew she was risking her very soul if she lied under oath and, in doing so, she might suffer eternal damnation in hell.

c. Laconnex

Laconnex, a village some eleven kilometers from the Genevan city walls, was located in contested territory claimed by Geneva, Bern, and Savoy. Laconnex was on the edge of the territory of St. Victor, a medieval clerical enclave conquered by the duke of Geneva in the fourteenth century. When, in the sixteenth century, the city of Geneva broke from the House of Savoy, the rebels continued to lay claim over St. Victor. In the meantime, Protestant Bern seized most of the lands around Geneva and also asserted authority over St. Victor. In principle, Genevan authorities could prosecute criminal activities that took place in St. Victor, but had to release criminals sentenced to death to Bern for the actual execution. On a number of occasions throughout the seventeenth century, these rules were bent or broken and caused diplomatic headaches between Geneva and Bern, and Geneva and Savoy. For Jeanne Catherine's trial, however, Bern ceded all authority to Geneva.

We know very little about the family who took care of Jeanne Catherine's daughter. Abraham Clerc was reported to be a laborer, which meant that he likely worked the land on seigneuries owned by local landowners, some of whom may have been based in Geneva, others not. The Clerc family had a history in Laconnex: Abraham's mother Louise had lived in Laconnex during her married life to Abraham's deceased father Étienne. Laborers were often paid by the day for specific tasks or could be contracted to a specific landowner for a period of time. In addition, Abraham may have owed some days each year in unpaid labor to local landowners. Abraham's earnings would have been modest and would have been supplemented by the food his wife cultivated in the garden plot beside their home, firewood gathered in nearby woods, and the cash earned by his wife as a wet nurse to a noble child.

We know that communities within Genevan territory sometimes issued formal complaints to the Small Council about judicial officials or clerics who had authority over and responsibilities to the village. Peasants had their own sense of honor and a powerful sense of what rights they enjoyed. Abusive officials sometimes drew their scorn and occasionally their disobedience. Genevan officials reciprocated by recognizing peasants as loyal subjects. The fact that Abraham and the other peasants who testified in the case against Jeanne Catherine were referred to as "honorable" in the court records is no accident. The Small Council took Abraham's accusation that someone had murdered his son very seriously and expended significant resources to try to discover the truth of the events in Laconnex.

The judicial official responsible for criminal matters in Laconnex was known as a *châtelain*. In 1686, the *châtelain* for St. Victor was Marc Sarasin, a young ambitious man in his thirties, member of one of the wealthiest families in Geneva. Marc Sarasin lived in Geneva and only visited Laconnex when duty required. This is indicated by his noting in his official report to the Small Council that he and his investigative team ventured as far as Laconnex on horseback, clearly at some inconvenience to themselves. Once there, Sarasin and the court clerk who accompanied him collected testimony individually from witnesses and other individuals who might have had knowledge of the alleged crime.

Witnesses gave their testimony orally, under oath, in the presence of the clerk and the *châtelain* only, not in public and not in a courtroom. The clerk listened to their statements and condensed them into a written form. Whereas the peasants would have been speaking a local dialect of Savoyard, the clerk translated their words into standard French. When reading these documents, it is important to remember that the clerk's wording is not literal; what he wrote down was always an interpretation of what had been said. Nevertheless, at the end of the interview, the clerk read what had been written out loud to the witness, and they confirmed that it was essentially correct. Even though the peasants could not read French, they probably understood it when read out loud. It was not unusual for early modern people living close to cities to be able to function aurally in several related dialects.

d. Court officers and criminal procedures

Geneva was a small enough city that residents knew where to turn if they witnessed a crime. One's first thought was likely to find an *auditeur*, a public investigator, whose role within Geneva itself was similar to that of a *châtelain* in the rural areas around the city. In the 1680s, there were six *auditeurs* in Geneva, and it seems people knew who they were. It was acceptable to go find the *auditeur* at home or visiting a friend. This is precisely what Abraham Clerc did when he arrived in Geneva in the late afternoon of Thursday, May 6th, dragging a reluctant Jeanne Catherine along with him. *Auditeurs* were the officials who did much of the legwork to determine whether a crime had been committed. They collected depositions from denouncers, suspects, and other witnesses; they gathered key circumstantial evidence at the scene of the crime; they conducted some if not all of the interrogations of suspects after their arrest. Unlike modern police officers, *auditeurs* were officials of the criminal court and were part of the prosecution team. As a result, from the first, a suspected criminal was faced with justifying their actions to a person whose job it was to prove their guilt.

In principle, *auditeurs* had the power to arrest suspects, although they were required to report their actions to the Small Council within twenty-four hours after having done so. When Jeanne Catherine was brought before the *auditeur*, Michel Humbert, on May 6th, he hesitated to arrest her on his own authority, however. This was because arresting a noblewoman was unusual. Like most criminal courts across early modern Europe, the vast majority of people accused and convicted of crimes in Geneva were commoners, usually members of the laboring or artisan classes. The Genevan court certainly possessed the authority to arrest anyone who might have committed a crime within its territory, but nobles, especially foreign nobles like Jeanne Catherine, were a special case. French nobles were often able to obtain an extradition request from the king of France, for example, and the Small Council aimed to avoid conflicts with its neighbors Savoy and Bern. As you will see, Humbert instead undertook a more complex process. His first move was to consult a lieutenant of justice.

The lieutenants of justice in 1686 were Jean de Normandie and Ami Lefort, well-respected men of the Genevan elite. Lieutenants were usually mature politicians who had long served on the Small Council and knew Genevan law and precedent well. This was essential because Genevan criminal statutes were brief and left much to the discretion of the judges. The lieutenants normally did very little of the day-to-day work of collecting evidence for a criminal trial. Instead, they collated what the *auditeurs* discovered and presented it to the Small Council to elicit the councillors' opinions regarding how best to proceed, as we will see in Jeanne Catherine's trial.

Unlike nearby France or the Holy Roman Empire (Germany) in which extensive bodies of legislation described key crimes and their required punishments in some detail, Geneva law assumed rather than defined many procedures. For example, neither the crimes of infanticide nor poisoning were described in local law statutes. The way that Genevan authorities prosecuted crimes was, however, very similar to how it was done in nearby Switzerland, Germany, and France. Criminal statutes in Western Europe at this time, including those in Geneva, relied heavily on an adapted version of imperial Roman law. This longstanding legal tradition emphasized the process of discovering truth over reconciling different parties in a conflict. Criminal prosecutions based on Roman law relied heavily on written evidence collected over a matter of days or weeks by clerks and *auditeurs*; this written evidence was presented to and evaluated by the judges, who only rarely heard the direct testimony of defendants aurally in court. Based on this documentation and consultations with the prosecutors, the judges then collectively decided whether the suspect was guilty.

The sometimes harsh punitive sentences imposed by early modern criminal courts, including flogging, banishment, and execution, were an indication of how weak the judicial systems of early modern European states actually were. This was in large measure because most jurisdictions did not have a regular police force whose main job it was to arrest suspects. Many criminals escaped prosecution by skipping out of town. In Geneva, one need not go far to reach Savoy, France, or the Vaud. In this trial, Daniel de la Fléchère, the cousin who accompanied Jeanne Catherine to Laconnex the day the children died, left Genevan territory later that afternoon. After having lunch with Jeanne Catherine in Geneva, he traveled home to Nyon along the north shore of Lake Geneva. Once he left Genevan territory and entered the Vaud in Switzerland, he could use his noble status to obtain protection from Genevan justice. Although governments communicated with one another about escaped suspects, formal extradition arrangements were rare. As a result, having fled a territory, one could usually remain free as long as one did not return to the place where one had been accused. After Jeanne Catherine's arrest, the Small Council sought to question Daniel about his possible role in the deaths of the children. As a result, the councillors wrote to the bailiff of Nyon to make that request.

In addition to criminal prosecution, it was also possible to launch civil suits in early modern Geneva. Abraham Clerc could have chosen to sue Jeanne Catherine for the death of his son. Had he done so and had her guilt been proven, he would have received a fiscal payment from Jeanne Catherine as compensation for the loss of his son. In his original deposition to the *auditeur*, however, Abraham made it clear that he was not seeking compensation; rather, he wished the Small Council to prosecute Jeanne Catherine's actions as a criminal matter. Recognizing that asking the Small Council to arrest a noblewoman like Jeanne Catherine was a tall order, Abraham offered to go to prison himself as a bond to Jeanne Catherine's arrest. This offer was a means of indicating the seriousness of his intentions. As far as we can tell, this would have been quite unusual, but so was arresting a noblewoman for suspected poisoning and infanticide.

Once the Small Council decided to arrest Jeanne Catherine, she was removed from the city hall and taken to a nearby prison. Genevan authorities housed prisoners in several locations in the city, most of them former church buildings. We do not know where she was imprisoned, but we know that she was held separately from her accusers, Abraham and his uncle, who, it seems, were only imprisoned a few days before being released.

In early modern Geneva, prisons were primarily holding tanks for suspects charged with crimes and awaiting trial. Criminal trials could last a few days, but, when the suspect was accused of a serious crime, it was not unusual for trials to drag on for several months. Conditions in the prison were generally harsh: stuffy in the summer, prisons were often bitterly cold in the winter. The standard food ration for prisoners was a simple bread and water diet, though families were welcome to leave additional food, clothing, and other objects for the prisoners. We know that members of Jeanne Catherine's family traveled to Geneva during the trial; possibly they brought food and other goods to make her more comfortable. Nevertheless, there is no question that spending time in prison in the seventeenth century was a punishment in itself. Jeanne Catherine was assigned an individual guard to watch her day and night. She would have had little privacy and would have known that her life was on the line. All told, she spent almost three months in prison, an experience that would have left her both physically and psychologically compromised.

Overall, criminal justice in early modern Europe was quite different from how crimes are prosecuted in North America today. Early modern defendants were not judged by a jury, but instead by a panel of judges. In early modern Geneva, this panel consisted of the twenty-five members of the Small Council, all elite men, most of whom had no formal training in the law. Instead, they relied on the prosecution team – the lieutenants and the *auditeurs* – to prove the guilt of the suspect. Suspects in the seventeenth century did not usually have access to a defense lawyer and were never formally informed of the charges against them. Suspects were only arrested once a significant amount of evidence was gathered against them and, as a result, the court did not assume that they were innocent until proven guilty. It was rather the opposite: the defendant was assumed to be guilty and the job of the prosecution was to prove it conclusively.

e. Proving a crime: Torture and punishment

Having decided to arrest Jeanne Catherine, the Small Council turned to the next order of business: gathering as much evidence as possible to establish her guilt. In order to achieve a "full proof" of a crime, Roman law, as interpreted by early modern judges, normally required that two respectable eyewitnesses testify or that the suspect(s) confess their guilt. But the court also accepted other forms of evidence. Circumstantial evidence such as weapons or corpses, eyewitness testimony by less than fully respectable individuals, testimony taken from other witnesses who may have seen something but not the crime itself, the suspect's good reputation or lack thereof, evidence provided by expert witnesses such as medical professionals – all of these lesser forms of evidence could establish a half proof of the crime, though in principle even a large number of these secondary forms of evidence could never fully prove that a crime had taken place. Once the court established a half proof, however, it could justify further interrogations of the suspect and even torture them with the hopes of obtaining the required confession. This system of proving crimes was actually more stringent than our system of proof today. Whereas our criminal courts prove the guilt of defendants "beyond a reasonable doubt," in principle early modern courts sought a definitive proof. This high burden of proof sometimes resulted in long, drawn-out criminal trials in which all means of proving the case were fully exploited.

Testimonies provided by witnesses were key pieces of evidence, both to establish a half proof and to provide detailed particulars with which to test the claims of innocence made by the suspect. In Jeanne Catherine's trial, most of the peasants involved in the affair were interviewed under oath in Laconnex, but a few key witnesses were called to Geneva to testify in court before an *auditeur* and a court clerk. The *auditeur* asked similar, ideally neutral, informative questions of all witnesses and tried to identify inconsistencies that might indicate someone was lying. In practice, *auditeurs* often asked leading questions and witnesses often told very similar stories. This may have been because the witnesses had all witnessed a crime and reported it accurately, but it was also likely the result of the way that news spread through a community. Even though witness testimony was in principle given in secret – witnesses were questioned alone by the *auditeur* and a clerk who wrote down their testimony and withheld it from prying eyes – the fact they had testified would be well known to their neighbors. Witnesses could be prosecuted for perjury if they reported false information, so they had to be careful to stick close to the truth or at least close to the story that they knew their neighbors would be presenting. They would know what their fellow neighbors were testifying because the adults in the community likely gossiped about the chain of events at some length before reporting it to authorities. In many trials, a suspected crime was only reported once the village or neighborhood reached a consensus about what had happened and who was to blame. It seems that this dynamic may have been at work in Jeanne Catherine's trial.

Both men and women served as witnesses, but female testimony usually required corroboration by a man. Because women were considered the weaker sex – weaker in body, mind, and spirit – a woman's word was, generally speaking, worth less in the courtroom than a man's. Nevertheless, if a woman was a respectable wife and mother and her husband, brother, or son could vouch for her, her testimony was still very much valued. In Jeanne Catherine's trial, Abraham Clerc and his uncle, neither of whom were present in Laconnex when the children fell ill, were chosen to report the alleged crime to the authorities. Even though they had little to offer in terms of eyewitness testimony, they could vouch for the reliability of the women of Laconnex who provided most of the detailed information. Female witnesses were certainly very important in trials in which women were the suspects and when the crime was a domestic one, i.e., one that occurred in the home or was related in some way to personal or sexual morality.

Circumstantial evidence, in this case medical evidence gleaned from the corpses of the children, was also a key element in many criminal trials, especially when the suspect was accused of poisoning. A wide variety of different kinds of medical professionals were called on to testify. Most prominent among them were surgeons and physicians. In early modern Europe, surgeons were not highly paid specialists as they are today, but were instead masters of a registered trade comparable to other artisans. As apprentices, surgeons-in-training received practical training in the home of a master surgeon who would teach them bloodletting, dental surgery, the removal of diseased limbs and even cutting hair, all the skills they needed to practice the trade. After years of such hands-on training, a journeyman surgeon was required to pass a set of exams set by the masters and then applied to the city for registration as a master surgeon in his own right.

On the other hand, physicians were university-trained professionals. Their medical credentials were not local but international: they had to prove they had attended and completed their medical training, for Genevan physicians usually at a university in France. Medical science in the seventeenth century still relied on the theories of classical Greek medicine, which emphasized a holistic understanding of good health often assessed by the movement of fluids such as bile, blood, and phlegm through the body. Although physicians in the seventeenth century were not aware of modern germ theory, they understood that some diseases were contagious and they sought physical explanations for illness and death. They had a deep, and what we would consider, mostly accurate knowledge of human anatomy, though their explanations for particular diseases were often very different from those provided by modern Western medicine. When consulting with a patient, their principal responsibility was to offer a diagnosis and propose healing regimens that often involved bloodletting, changing the patient's diet, and taking medications that might purge dangerous blockages of bodily fluids and restore balance to the system.

Physicians often prescribed medicines and thus worked closely with apothecaries, trained specialists who prepared herbs and chemical compounds and sold them. The apothecary profession was a practical trade like surgery, and apothecaries were often summoned to testify during criminal trials. They were usually asked whether they had sold a particular substance to a suspected individual since many compounds that could kill, such as arsenic and lead, were sometimes combined with herbs and used as remedies during the early modern period. At the end of Jeanne Catherine's trial, a local apothecary was questioned about whether he had sold her poison the day before the children died.

In Jeanne Catherine's trial, the corpses of the two children provided key medical evidence. As a result, a team of surgeons and physicians was sent out to Laconnex to examine their bodies. Both the surgeons and the physicians reported on what they found. The physicians also provided a second report to the court. In it, they described in some detail the chemical experiments they conducted on a granular substance they claimed to have found in the stomach of the five-year-old boy who died. They asserted that this granular substance was a pure form of poison, which defies our modern understanding of how a poison would be digested and absorbed into the body. In an effort to be systematic and unbiased in their analysis, they undertook controlled experiments, blending the substance with known chemicals. In doing so, the physicians were seeking to demonstrate their professional credentials as men of science. By the late seventeenth century, a European culture of experimental scientists was developing. In 1667, the king of France established a Royal Society of Sciences composed of learned men who met regularly to discuss the experimental scientific method and to share their research. They also produced printed publications with much wider circulation. Although it is highly unlikely that the physicians who testified in Jeanne Catherine's case would ever have attended these meetings in Paris, they were clearly well-aware of the burgeoning debates about how best to obtain consistent experimental results. Their detailed description of their experiments aimed to demonstrate the impartiality of their methods and, as a result, the absolute certainty of their scientific conclusions.

Unquestionably, the most important piece of evidence in any early modern criminal trial was the testimony provided by the suspect. A credible confession made by the defendant that matched the other evidence already collected in the trial proved their guilt. As a result, getting the suspect to confess was a major preoccupation of the court. Defendants were occasionally interrogated in the chamber where the Small Council sat in front of the councillors; most, however, were interrogated elsewhere, either elsewhere in the courthouse or in the prison. Once torture was authorized, defendants were brought to a chamber where the torture instruments were located to be questioned in the presence of an *auditeur*, a clerk, the executioner (who undertook any torture procedures), and sometimes a medical professional. Because defendants were not accompanied to interrogations by a defense lawyer and were not told what charges had been laid against them, suspects could only guess from the interrogator's questions what they were being accused of. Councillors hoped for a quick confession, which would render the trial short, thus saving public funds for other expenses (criminal prosecutions were paid for out of the public purse). Defendants who resisted confessing were often characterized as "obstinate" or "hardened against God" because interrogators already assumed they were likely to be guilty. This prejudice tended to intensify over the course of the trial as more witness testimony and circumstantial evidence were gathered. This perspective was often reflected in the questions that interrogators posed to suspects.

If the circumstantial evidence was weak, the Small Council could dismiss the case and set the defendant free. In Jeanne Catherine's case, however, the testimonies of the witnesses and reports of the physicians were considered damning. As a result, the councillors decided to test Jeanne Catherine's claims to innocence in a judicial ritual called a "confrontation."

Jeanne Catherine was confronted in person with the wet nurse's mother-in-law, Louise Ducré, the most important witness for the prosecution. The confrontation provided an opportunity for the defendant and the witness to look each other in the eye while trying to maintain their version of the truth before the judges. This was also an opportunity for Jeanne Catherine to argue that the witness was biased against her personally or to assert that she had lied under oath.

Interrogators were also willing to torture suspects. By the 1680s, torture was a well-established judicial practice in Geneva and so its use in Jeanne Catherine's trial should not surprise us. Across Western Europe, jurisdictions that relied heavily on Roman law traditions acknowledged the validity of using physical pain to try to elicit a confession of guilt. Nevertheless, the vast majority of criminal defendants in Geneva and elsewhere in Europe were not tortured; torture was instead mostly reserved for individuals accused of horrible crimes including premeditated theft, treason, heresy, arson, and murder. Torture was considered a valid means of extracting the truth "from the mouth of the accused" because it was hemmed in by a number of procedures that tried to correct for the possibility of defendants lying to escape the pain.

First, interrogators did their best to try to get the suspect to confess without having to apply pain. Once the Small Council approved the use of torture against a particular defendant, the suspect was first interrogated in the presence of the torture instruments, but not attached to them, as a warning of what would await them if they refused to confess. The next stage was to attach the defendant to the torture instruments and explicitly threaten torture. This was often enough to elicit a confession and such confessions were considered more reliable than confessions made under pain. Councillors understood that torture was a risky tool that sometimes produced false information.

On the other hand, as Christians, court officials also believed that pain could purify the soul and allow an individual to confess openly before God. Early modern Christians believed that Christ's painful sacrifice on the cross was a deeply spiritual act and they emphasized the significance of the physical pain that Christ experienced as he was crucified. Seventeenth-century Protestant writings on illness and death taught the faithful that pain was a gift from God, a test that allowed them to suffer like Christ. In identifying with Christ, a faithful Christian could purify their soul and prepare themselves for the afterlife. The behavior of court officials in Geneva suggests that they saw the pain of torture as a test that had particular spiritual resonance and could bring the defendant, even if they were guilty, closer to God. If the suspect confessed their crimes, they had a chance of obtaining absolution from God. Interrogators often asked defendants pointed questions about the state of their consciences before they were tortured and insisted that they reflect on their relationship with God as pain was applied. Suspects understood that what they said under torture would have a direct impact on whether they were likely to be executed. More importantly, they understood that lying under torture could cost them any chance of attaining eternal salvation. Thus, even though everyone knew that a person could lie under torture, both court officials and suspects understood that doing so could be very costly. The high value placed on confessions under torture is indicated by the fact that the words spoken by Jeanne Catherine while in pain were transcribed in direct quotations and written down in the first person (rather than in the third person, which was the norm for most interrogations). Torture sessions were an opportunity for the suspect to confess directly before God.

In preparation for a torture session, defendants were stripped down to a loose undershirt, and their bodies were rigorously searched for fear that they hid a magical amulet or charm on their bodies that would protect them from pain. Some defendants' heads were shaved, both to humiliate them and to find suspect objects hidden in their hair. By the seventeenth century, the most common forms of torture in Geneva were the *corde* and the *estrapade*. These both involved tying the hands of the suspect behind their back and lifting them off the ground on a pulley system by their wrists. If subjected to the *corde*, the defendant was lifted and left to hang for a period of time. This inevitably caused intense pain in their arms and shoulders. If this first stage did not elicit a confession, the Small Council sometimes authorized the *estrapade*, in which the suspect, still lifted off the ground, was then sharply dropped just shy of the floor. This operation usually dislocated the shoulders of the defendant, resulting in an intense pain that often prevented them from speaking. When a defendant confessed under torture, their confession was duly recorded by the clerk, along with their screams and appeals for mercy. They were then detached from the instruments and taken back to the prison to recover.

The next day they were returned to the torture chamber and questioned again about what they had confessed – this time without using torture. Exhausted and fearing more torture, the suspect normally reaffirmed their confession of guilt, though a small minority of defendants recanted, claiming that their confession under torture was all lies. This usually resulted in additional torture sessions. Unlike in Germany and in France, there was no legal limit on the number of times that an individual could be tortured in early modern Geneva, though in practice, by the late seventeenth century, suspects were rarely tortured more than once and almost never more than three times. Once Jeanne Catherine refused to confess three times under torture, her family did not hesitate to write to the Small Council to demand that the torture cease. Torture was waning as a judicial practice in the late seventeenth century and Jeanne Catherine was among the last suspects to receive the "full torture" of the *estrapade*.

If an individual persisted in maintaining their innocence under torture, the Small Council had an additional strategy they sometimes used to try to encourage defendants to confess. Protestant ministers were sent to visit the defendant in private between formal interrogations to urge them to confess all their sins before God. In doing so, the ministers had a spiritual mission to bring the defendant closer to God, with the added benefit that a criminal would thus be revealed to the court. The Small Council repeatedly tried this approach with Jeanne Catherine who continued to maintain her innocence.

If a suspect absolutely refused to confess their guilt under torture or during a private session with a minister, the court had three options. The first was to drop all charges against them and set them free. The Small Council chose this path fairly regularly in the late sixteenth century, particularly when women were accused of witchcraft and refused to confess. But this practice, called purgation (because the failure to obtain a confession under torture purged all other evidence in the case), gradually fell out of use in the seventeenth century. A second, more commonplace, option was to reduce the sentence from execution to banishment. This was considered the best solution when the court deemed the circumstantial evidence to be strong, but the definitive guilt of the suspect could not be proven. The third option was to execute the suspect anyway, even though they had not confessed. In cases in which the circumstantial evidence was very strong and the crime particularly horrifying, the Small Council sometimes ruled that guilt was "sufficiently proven." Even though the councillors recognized that a full proof had not been established, this phrase indicated that they had decided that the other evidence in the trial was persuasive enough to make a confession superfluous.

Because torture was reserved for serious crimes only, both torture and execution were relatively exceptional procedures in Geneva at the end of the seventeenth century. Most serious crimes were punished with banishment: in 1650, for example, sixteen individuals accused of serious crimes received a final sentence of banishment and only one individual was executed. Between 1650 and 1700, the Genevan Small Council issued the death sentence against eighty-nine individuals. Most of these individuals escaped execution, however. Fifty-one of them (57 per cent) were executed in effigy: that is to say, a stuffed straw replica of the individual was "killed" instead. These executions by effigy were the result of suspects who failed to be arrested before they fled Genevan territory. A much smaller number, eight individuals, escaped death because they appealed their final sentences to a higher court, the Council of Two Hundred, and were either pardoned or received a mitigated sentence. Thus, all told, only thirty individuals were actually executed in the flesh, less than one execution per year. By the second half of the seventeenth century, the Small Council was increasingly reluctant to execute criminals especially if they refused to confess their guilt.

As in the rest of Europe in the early modern period, executions were public affairs. Executions took place in public to deter the common folk from following in the path of criminals and to signal the dangers of breaking the law (for those who were caught). The criminal was stripped to their undershirt and either taken on a cart or forced to walk through the city streets in view of the whole community on their way to the site of execution. In Geneva, the two sites of execution were just outside the city walls, in Champel and in Plainpalais, where permanent scaffolds were erected. Criminals were accompanied by officers of the court, sometimes by an armed guard (mostly to keep the peace and prevent onlookers from disrupting the execution), and by Protestant ministers ready to offer them spiritual consolation. Criminals were urged to call out, begging for forgiveness from God for their sins and from the Small Council for the crimes they committed. This procession would have been particularly shameful for convicted criminals of noble status. Stripped of the clothing that marked them as honorable and deserving of respect, they were reduced to a common denominator: the sinful Christian who had abandoned God and was likely going to hell. Once they arrived at the execution site, some criminals loudly proclaimed their innocence and complained about the injustice of the criminal prosecution in their last dying speeches, but the vast majority toed the line and proclaimed their guilt publicly one last time.

Even criminals who had refused to confess under torture sometimes admitted their guilt at the scaffold. Faced with the grim reality of their imminent death, some criminals may have realized that they would suffer eternal damnation should they not admit their sins to God. Others may have falsely claimed they committed the crime because they wanted to protect a third party from prosecution. Others feared that their executions would be made more painful and drawn-out if they did not produce the required confession.

The most common forms of execution in late seventeenth-century Geneva were hanging and beheading. Hanging was the default method and was usually conducted on a simple scaffold in which the individual was swung off a ladder to hang by the neck. Death was not immediate but rather resulted from suffocation. It was a messy, painful, and prolonged affair. In contrast, beheading was supposed to be quick and, as a result, was usually the method reserved for citizens, *bourgeois*, and nobles. Although in practice it took a lot of skill to chop off someone's head with a single blow, it was hoped that beheading would result in a more efficient, less humiliating, death. Afterward, the corpses of criminals normally remained displayed on the scaffold, left to rot as an example to the general public of the cost of sin. Sometimes, as a concession to their high social status, the corpses of citizen and noble criminals were removed from the execution site. Criminals could not be buried in the churchyard since they were confirmed sinners, but their bodies could be returned to their family for private burial or were sometimes buried near the site of the execution.

f. Good mothers and bad mothers

Marriage and motherhood were considered the life goal of all Protestant women. Girls were trained from a young age to prepare themselves for motherhood and for their duties as a wife. Depending on their social status, this training might be very different. Women of the noble class like Jeanne Catherine received more instruction in household management and the disciplining of servants whereas the daughter of an artisan learned how to keep a modest household and bargain for cheap food at the market. All girls were taught to sew and some to embroider in order to start making key items for their trousseau, household linens and clothes they would bring to the marriage as part of their dowry. Girls were also trained to be good Christians who would protect their virtue, meaning their virginity, until marriage so that husbands would only support children that they had themselves sired and the girls would keep their good reputation. Even though it was commonplace for couples to start having sex once they were betrothed, doing so was always a risk and it was the woman who paid the higher cost if things did not work out as planned.

Motherhood within marriage was thought to be the pinnacle of female experience. Women were taught to hope for many children and were shamed (and blamed) should they fail to produce offspring. Although both parents were responsible for the moral upbringing of children, women were expected to provide the initial grounding in Christian teachings when the children were small. Respectable motherhood provided women with status and power both within the family and the community since they were manifestly contributing to its welfare by providing a new generation of good Christians and productive workers. Raising healthy children

Woodcut of woman giving birth with midwife
Prints and Photographs Collection, History of Medicine Division, National
Library of Medicine.

to adulthood was a challenge that required vigilance, prayer, and a good
deal of luck.

Even though most women worked hard at the family business or in
other occupations, all married mothers relied on the economic support
of their husbands to raise their children. Men had much greater earn-
ing potential and were legally and financially responsible for the material
well-being of the household. Having children was both a huge investment
and a huge risk for couples. Because birth control was difficult to access and
unreliable, most couples started having children as soon as they married or
even before (many betrothed couples married once the bride became pregnant) and continued doing so until someone died or the wife reached about
forty years of age. The spacing of births depended on whether the family
employed a wet nurse or not. The laboring poor could not afford a wet nurse
and kept their children at home. People knew that nursing a child could
suppress fertility in women; mothers who nursed (and may themselves have

been malnourished) tended to have children less frequently, usually every two to three years. Many married mothers in seventeenth-century Geneva, however, chose not to nurse their own children. Women of the artisanal class were needed in household workshops and so sent their infants out to nurse in the villages around Geneva some six weeks after birth. This choice tended to decrease the spacing between births: a mother who did not nurse her infant might find herself pregnant a few months later.

Rural wet nurses were usually married peasant women who had recently weaned a child of their own and sought to supplement the family income by caring for other people's children. Elite women in Geneva also employed wet nurses, though they usually recruited nurses who were willing to live in the birth mother's home where the family could keep an eye on the care they provided for the infant. Infants cared for at home had better survival rates, but not by a huge margin. Parish records indicate that mortality for all children was very high. In Geneva, 50 per cent of children died before the age of ten in the seventeenth century, with up to half of those deaths occurring in the first year of life. Among those children sent to the local orphanage or to a rural wet nurse, the death rate was higher again.

Even though children often died young in early modern Europe, this did not mean that they were not loved. Some families may have held back from emotionally bonding with the child at first and waited to baptize the child until they survived the first vulnerable weeks of life. Once they were sent out to nurse, however, many parents remained concerned about their well-being, reporting in personal account books about the good health of the child and expressing distress when they did not survive. It is hard to know how often parents visited their children who were put out to nurse, but the fact that Jeanne Catherine had visited her daughter on a number of occasions seemed notable to contemporaries. The fact that Jeanne Catherine sent her daughter out to wet nurse was not unusual. As a noblewoman, she probably never expected to nurse her own children. The fact that she chose a rural wet nurse rather than a live-in one had everything to do with her legally ambivalent status as a single mother.

Many women never married: as many as 20 per cent of women in Geneva remained single in the late seventeenth century. If they were members of relatively wealthy families, they continued to live with their families and were expected to care for ill parents even as they were also considered burdens to the family. If they were from poorer families in the villages surrounding Geneva, however, they usually had to leave home to work, most commonly as servants but also in the burgeoning textile industry. Once they left home, young women were vulnerable to seduction or rape by employers or by men of their own social class. Some men convinced them to have sex by promising to marry them once they became pregnant. Young women often appealed to the Genevan consistory to complain that their sexual partner had betrayed a promise to marry them and to try to get the court to pressure the men to do so. Sometimes pregnant young women and their families were successful in pressuring the sexual partner to do the right thing.

What about the women who failed to convince their sexual partners to marry them, perhaps because he was too poor or perhaps because he was already married? These were the "bad mothers" of early modern Geneva. Most of them were members of the poor working class and they usually lost their jobs once their employer realized they were pregnant. Without a regular income and with no prospects, these young women had few options and society judged them harshly, more so in Geneva than in some nearby German and French cities. Having had sex out of wedlock (a sin) and having failed to secure marriage from an upstanding man who would take responsibility for his children, these single mothers were disciplined and sometimes banished from the city.

Surprisingly, however, Genevan authorities also sometimes supported the mothers' efforts to raise their children. Pregnant single mothers in Geneva could sue for paternity support. This was such a common practice that the *auditeur* queried Jeanne Catherine at one point why she had not come to the authorities to request paternity support for her illegitimate daughter. The willingness of the Genevan Small Council to prosecute some fathers was the flipside of their judgment of extramarital sex as a serious sin: even though women were judged more harshly, the court recognized that men should also be held responsible for their actions. The father was usually required to pay a sum of money to the local orphanage to cover the costs of the child's maintenance and the mother was expected to leave the child in its care.

Pregnant single women were strongly encouraged to leave Geneva before the baby was born. This was because city authorities felt more responsible for children born in the city than they did for infants born elsewhere – most babies born outside the city had no right to be left at the orphanage. Widows in Geneva were forbidden from renting rooms to single women who were pregnant and midwives were fined for helping single mothers to give birth. Midwives in Geneva were a regulated profession like surgeons and apothecaries. They were responsible for reporting illegitimate mothers to the authorities and were required to find out the name of the father of the bastard child from the mother during childbirth. As a result, like Jeanne Catherine, most single mothers left the city to give birth. Most had their children in one of the nearby villages where they found local peasant women willing to take them in (at a price). Note that all of the women involved in the birth of Jeanne Catherine's daughter in Laconnex were at pains to report to the *auditeur* that they had tried to discover the name of the father of her child. In doing so, they were hoping to avoid being prosecuted for having illegally helped Jeanne Catherine. It is clear that respectable married women regularly helped single mothers like Jeanne Catherine give birth and support their children. As long as they were paid for their services, village women had no qualms about doing so, that is, as long as the health and well-being of their own children were not put at risk.

g. Prosecuting poisoning and infanticide

During the sixteenth and seventeenth centuries, thousands of women across Western Europe were prosecuted for having murdered their infants or young children. Most of these women were poor and unmarried. Historians argue that they may have neglected or deliberately killed their children due to the shame of being an unwed mother. More likely, they knew that they could not support their children without a husband and did not know where to turn. Although infanticide was not a new phenomenon in early modern Europe, we know more about the fate of these young mothers because they were prosecuted more vigorously after 1550 than in previous centuries. New legislation promulgated in France, Germany, and England between 1530 and 1630 made it easier to convict young single mothers who gave birth to illegitimate children secretly and whose infants then mysteriously died. In principle, just the fact of having hidden the birth and the death from prying eyes was sufficient grounds for criminal prosecution and even conviction.

Not surprisingly, even though no such statute regarding infanticide existed in Genevan law, the bloodiest period for its prosecution in Geneva also occurred during the seventeenth century. The Small Council was suspicious of many infant deaths that occurred within married households or when babies died in the care of wet nurses, but the only individuals prosecuted with the full force of the law were single mothers, women who had their children out of wedlock, hid the pregnancy, and then were suspected of having killed the child in Geneva. These young mothers were subject to imprisonment and tough interrogation techniques, including torture, to find out whether they had deliberately planned to kill their child. Medical evidence was crucial to these investigations; in the case of infant deaths, both the suspected mother and the corpse of the infant were examined. When it was established that the death of the child had been caused by physical trauma (most commonly strangling or bleeding out from failing to tie the umbilical cord but sometimes poison), the authorities sometimes tortured the suspected mother to obtain a confession of guilt. In other cases, however, the medical evidence discovered during the investigation could raise questions about whether the single mother had actually intended the child to die. When the baby was born premature, when the mother abandoned the child but did not harm the child physically, when the infant seemed to have died of natural causes, the authorities sometimes gave these young mothers the benefit of the doubt. Ten of the twenty-eight single mothers prosecuted for infanticide in seventeenth-century Geneva received mitigated sentences such as flogging or banishment because it could not absolutely be proven that they had intended to kill their infant. The other eighteen women were executed.

The trial of Jeanne Catherine was not a typical infanticide prosecution. First of all, she was noble. The vast majority of single mothers accused of infanticide were servants and women of the working poor who had been seduced with the promise of marriage or financial support. These women had very few resources: often immigrants from nearby rural villages, they were living alone in the city isolated from social and familial networks that might have shielded them from the law. In contrast, Jeanne Catherine had some access to funds to support her daughter and a family that was willing to advocate on her behalf.

Secondly, Jeanne Catherine's child was not a vulnerable infant but a baptized two-year-old who was well-known in Laconnex. The age of the child was important because of high natural rates of death among infants. On some level, people expected that infants might die and the community probably did not invest much emotional commitment in them. A named child who was healthy and thriving at age two was, on the other hand, a precious being who needed to be given every chance to survive the remaining hazards of childhood. It seems that everyday Genevans were more horrified by the murder of an older child than that of an infant.

Finally, it was significant that her daughter had died in Laconnex, outside the city walls, and that another child had died at the same time. Genevan authorities were much less interested in suspicious deaths of infants that occurred away from the city. In 1675, the Genevan authorities received a report that a former servant named Jeanne Mestral had become pregnant by her master in Geneva. Before giving birth, she left Geneva to return to her home village of Laconnex and then had left Laconnex to give birth nearby where her father was employed as a farm laborer. The baby died some months later. The *châtelain* reported that Jeanne had "lost her child to poison and then buried it in the garden" and that Jeanne had then fled.[1] The Small Council could have prosecuted Jeanne Mestral for poisoning or

---

[1] Archives d'État de Genève (AEG), Registres du Consistoire 62, f. 22 (April 1, 1675).

infanticide. Instead, the authorities chose to interview the alleged father who denied paternity and expressed no interest in the fate of the child. As a result, the Small Council did nothing at all. This was not unusual. Every year in the 1670s and 1680s, single mothers returned to Geneva after giving birth in the countryside, without their children. They quickly found work as servants or as wet nurses in elite families. Sometimes they explained that their babies had died, and their explanations were accepted at face value, which would not have been the case had their child died within the city itself. Sometimes they claimed that the baby was being cared for by a wet nurse, though it is not clear how they, as servants, could afford to pay for its upkeep. Generally speaking, Genevan authorities were willing to turn a blind eye to babies abandoned or possibly killed in the countryside. Had only little Jeanne died on May 6, 1686, quite possibly the Genevan authorities would have shown little interest in her death. An unknown illegitimate child who died in the care of a wet nurse would not have raised many eyebrows in early modern Geneva. It was only because the son of the Clerc family also died and his parents sought to blame someone for his death that criminal prosecution was initiated.

Like the servant Jeanne Mestral, Jeanne Catherine was accused of poisoning rather than of infanticide. Poisoning was not an exclusively female crime, but it was often associated with women. Women, after all, prepared meals for their family and were thought to prefer non-violent means of ending the life of their victims or enemies. Poisoning was considered one of the most heinous forms of murder possible. It was dishonorable since the victim had no opportunity to defend themselves. It was deliberate and premeditated since one had to obtain the poison and then decide, sometimes repeatedly in the case of slow poisoning by arsenic, to introduce it into the food of the victim. It was also considered the ultimate betrayal since the victim was almost always someone the murderer knew well and who trusted them. It was also very difficult to prove. Prosecutors usually sought evidence that poison had been purchased and aimed to prove poisoning based on the symptoms of the victims and the confession of the accused.

If a woman was found guilty of infanticide or of poisoning in early modern Geneva, it was not inevitable that she would be executed. If a female convict enjoyed high social status, her male relatives might appeal the final sentence with the hopes of obtaining a pardon from the Genevan Council of Two Hundred, the only appeals council in the city. These appeals were relatively unusual, but a few did occur in the late seventeenth century. In making these appeals, women were much more likely to receive a sympathetic hearing if men in their family, normally their fathers or husbands, put in a good word on their behalf. In 1690, Jeanne

Marie Fontaine was found guilty of having attempted to poison her mother-in-law, but her birth family, based in Lausanne, sought to appeal the death sentence issued against her. Jeanne Marie was doomed by the fact that her own husband, a respectable Genevan resident, was sufficiently convinced of her guilt that he banished her from his home before the trial even began. Not surprisingly, the appeal failed and Jeanne Marie was hanged.[2] In the 1672 trial of Marie Mercier for infanticide, however, the impassioned appeal of her father, François Mercier, a well-established citizen and tailor, seemed to have swayed the Small Council. François Mercier offered considerable deference to the councillors, addressing them as "magnificent, very honorable, and governing Lords"[3] and referred to himself as their "very humble and very obedient servant." Even though he expressed profound respect for the final sentence they had issued against his daughter, execution by beheading, he humbly requested that they reconsider whether the harsh punishment was warranted. Marie had been found guilty of having given birth to an illegitimate child and then having abandoned it in the city streets where it had died. He argued that his daughter Marie was a young woman of good reputation: she had never caused any trouble and had never been summoned to the church court for bad behavior and that her actions immediately following the birth had been taken out of fear not premeditation. Though couched in pious Christian rhetoric and a request for mercy, Mercier's letter also made a crucial legal point: his daughter had not directly harmed her infant and had instead panicked when she abandoned it. The court had not proven that she planned to murder her child or had deliberately caused its death. This approach was successful. The capital sentence against Marie was reduced to confinement in the Genevan house of correction, with a special concession that she be lodged in a separate room.[4] Even though being found guilty of poisoning or infanticide put defendants at significant risk, it was possible for them to escape with their life even when the Small Council decided that they had done the deed.

II. UNDERSTANDING THE TEXT

The criminal trial of Jeanne Catherine Thomasset is an exceptional resource. Although we know that thousands of women were prosecuted for infanticide and poisoning in early modern Europe, relatively few complete trials survive. Pests, fire, neglect, water damage, and outright destruction

---

[2] AEG Procès Criminels 1e Série 4824.
[3] AEG Procès Criminels 1e Série 4212.
[4] AEG Recueil du Conseil (RC) 172, f. 229 (May 29, 1672).

have consigned most documents from the seventeenth century to dust. The state archives in Geneva are, however, both more comprehensive and detailed than most collections when it comes to early modern history. The criminal archives contain over four thousand criminal trials from the 1500–1700 period, an incredibly rich treasure trove of information. Many trials are short, but a minority offer historians detailed information that is unavailable at other archives. The discovery of the trial of Jeanne Catherine allows us to analyze the trial from multiple angles and extrapolate from her experience to the kinds of challenges faced by single mothers accused of infanticide in other parts of Europe.

a. The archival source

The trial of Jeanne Catherine Thomasset can be found in the state archives of the modern canton of Geneva (AEG, Procès Criminels, 1e Série 4694). The documents are grouped together in a single large folder, an arrangement that occurred centuries later when the criminal records were reorganized, labeled, and inventoried. The documents are mostly in chronological order, with the exception that documents not generated by the *auditeurs* and their clerks, such as personal letters between Jeanne Catherine and her kin and letters received from Swiss officials, were tucked into the end of the dossier. Other documents seminal to the proceedings are not included in the file at all, specifically the daily records of the Small Council can be found in a different archival series (Recueil du Conseil). Because the Small Council was responsible for prosecuting Jeanne Catherine and rendering a final sentence, these deliberations have been included here.

All of the documents have been rearranged into chronological order. This allows the modern reader to gather the information of the case as the court officials did, day by day, piece by piece. As noted earlier, when reading the trial of Jeanne Catherine, we need to remain attentive to the partial nature of the records. Even though we have ample information here to reveal many important aspects of the trial, we will never know for certain what is missing that might shed a different light on these events.

b. Notes on the translation

The original documents were all written in a fairly standard form of seventeenth-century French, the language of record for the Small Council and other Genevan political councils. We should not assume, however, that everyone involved in the case spoke this same kind of French. Notably, the peasants of Laconnex would have spoken a local Savoyard dialect. It was common practice at this time to translate the testimony of people speaking a dialect into a more regularized form. We should thus be aware that testimony offered here was not verbatim but an interpretation of the language the clerk heard. You will also note that the clerk copied testimony in the third person rather than the first person: "she did this" rather than "I did this." This awkward formulation has been left in the translation to remind readers that all court records are documents that have been shaped for the purposes of proving the innocence or guilt of the accused.

Seventeenth-century written French is largely similar to modern French, but punctuation habits have changed considerably. Early modern readers were far more accustomed to long sentences that might address several different subjects within a single frame. Although on some occasions longer sentences were left intact in this translation, in others the sentences have been broken up for ease of reading. Differences between language usage among the different genres of documents in the file have been retained. The language employed during interrogations is presented here as simple and direct and the replies of witnesses and Jeanne Catherine are similarly short, pointed, and fairly straightforward. In contrast, the language in the personal and official letters included in the file is more formal, suggestive, and often ambiguous.

The names of places and persons and all dates have been modernized and standardized, with the exception that double-barreled first names have been left without a hyphen (i.e., Jeanne Catherine rather than Jeanne-Catherine). Passages in the documents are sometimes damaged or illegible. When several words are unreadable, this is indicated by an ellipsis in square brackets [...].

III. LIST OF IMPORTANT CHARACTERS

Abraham Clerc	farm laborer in Laconnex, wife was nursing Jeanne Catherine's daughter, complainant in the trial
Antoine Léger	Protestant minister, professor of philosophy and natural sciences
Benjamin Noël	coroner, surgeon
Claudine Girard	woman in whose home Jeanne Catherine gave birth
Daniel de la Fléchère	cousin of Jeanne Catherine, living in Nyon
Daniel Le Clerc	physician who examined corpses of the children
Dominique Beddevole	physician who examined corpses of the children
Étienne Demonthoux	surgeon who examined corpses of the children

Étienne Dentand	surgeon who examined corpses of the children
François Joly	court clerk for Laconnex
François Turretini	Protestant minister, professor of theology and former principal of the Genevan Academy
Gabriel Cramer	physician who examined Samuel Thomasset
Gabriel Régis	cousin of Jeanne Catherine who paid wet nurse
Galiffe	court clerk in Geneva
Gédéon Régis	cousin of Jeanne Catherine who paid wet nurse
Gilbert Deromieux	apothecary living in Avully
Jacob François Margel	brother-in-law of Jeanne Catherine
Jacquema Mery	midwife at the birth of Jeanne Catherine's daughter
Jean François Thomasset	father of Jeanne Catherine, living in Agiez
Jean Pierre Bagueret	*auditeur*
Jean Robert Choüet	professor of science, member of Small Council
Jeanne Catherine Thomasset	accused of poisoning two children
Jeanne Marie Favre	wife of Abraham Clerc, mother of dead boy, wet nurse to Jeanne Catherine's daughter
Jeanne Thomasset	illegitimate daughter of Jeanne Catherine
Jeanne Vautier	Jeanne Catherine's landlady in Geneva
Joanne de la Fléchère	cousin of Jeanne Catherine
Jonas Roch	father of Jeanne Catherine's illegitimate child, living in Orbe
Louis Tronchin	Protestant minister
Louise Ducré	mother of Abraham Clerc, grandmother of dead boy
Marc Sarasin	*châtelain*, public investigator of St. Victor where Laconnex is located
Melchisédec Pinault	Protestant minister
Michel Humbert	*auditeur*
Nicolas Steiguer	bailiff of Nyon in the Vaud region of Switzerland
Pernette	servant employed by Jeanne Catherine's landlady

Pierre Favre	brother of Jeanne Marie Favre, living in Avully
Pierre Fabri	mayor of Geneva, brother-in-law of Jeanne Catherine's landlady the widow Fabri
Pierre Favre	brother of the wet nurse Jeanne Marie Favre
Pierre Perdriau	*auditeur*
Pierre Quiby	uncle of Abraham Clerc
Pierre Roy	apothecary in Geneva
Pierre Seure	personal guard for Jeanne Catherine in jail
Romier Laisné	relative of Jeanne Catherine
Samuel Thomasset	brother of Jeanne Catherine
Théodore Vautier	Protestant minister of Cartigny
Widow Fabri	aka Jeanne Vautier, sister of Théodore Vautier, sister-in-law of the mayor of Geneva

IV. GLOSSARY

apothecary	druggist who mixes chemical compounds and sells them
bailiff	chief judicial and military official in a district (*bailliage*) of the Vaud region
auditeur	public criminal investigator in Geneva
châtelain	public criminal investigator in the rural territories of Geneva
clerk	court official responsible for writing down the testimony of deponents, suspects, and the decisions made by the Small Council
corde	torture technique in which the hands of the suspect are tied behind their back and the suspect is raised on a pulley system by their wrists and left to hang
coroner	officer of the court responsible for examining suspicious corpses
councillor	elite Genevan man elected to the Small Council
Damoiselle	honorific title like "Madam" to indicate a woman of high social status, either married or unmarried
deponent	person who provides testimony under oath
écu	currency denomination worth 20 *florins* or 240 *sols* or 2880 *deniers* (the least valuable

écu (cont'd)	Genevan currency). Average daily wage in Geneva for a male laborer was approximately 10–24 *sols* per day, thus it would take a male day laborer ten to twenty days of work to earn one *écu*
estrapade	most painful torture technique in Geneva, commonplace in Europe; individual is raised and then dropped sharply from a pulley system with hands tied behind the back
honorable	title indicating the respectable status of either a man or a woman
lieutenant	officer of Small Council responsible for supervising the *auditeurs* and *châtelains*
Messieurs	more than one Monsieur, plural honorific
Monsieur	honorific title like "sir" to indicate a man of high social status
orviétan	medical compound of herbs and chemicals designed to purge poisons and employed as a general cure-all, found in most households
physician	university-trained medical doctor
seigneur	large-scale rural landowner who usually enjoyed labor rights over some of the peasants living on the land or nearby and had the right to be paid local fees by those peasants
Sieur	honorific title like "Monsieur" to indicate a man of high social status
Small Council	an elected council of twenty-five elite men responsible for executive and judicial matters in Geneva
surgeon	a medical professional authorized to conduct autopsies and surgeries
syndic	one of the four executive officers of the Small Council
thériaque	similar to *orviétan*
witness	individual summoned to provide testimony in a criminal trial, questioned privately by an *auditeur* and a court clerk

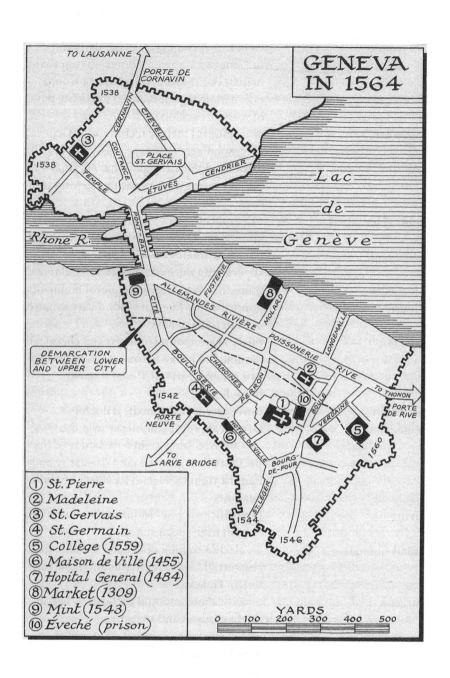

Map of Geneva

Calvin's Geneva, John Wiley and Sons.

The Trial

--- **FOLIO 1** ---

[May 6, 1686. This document was written by Auditeur (public investigator) Michel Humbert, a trained lawyer and a longstanding government official. Humbert was the first official to hear the declaration made against Noble Jeanne Catherine Thomasset, accused of having poisoned two children in the village of Laconnex, eleven kilometers outside of the city. In this first report, Humbert heard testimony from Abraham Clerc, father of the dead boy, Jeanne Catherine, and Jeanne Catherine's landlady, referred to here as the widow Fabri, but whose name was Jeanne Vautier. Women usually kept their maiden names in seventeenth-century Geneva. Jeanne Vautier was a respectable widow, sister-in-law to the mayor of Geneva. The mayor, Pierre Fabri, a seventy-year-old citizen and landowner, was also consulted regarding the possibility of arresting Jeanne Catherine.]

I, Michel Humbert, certify that, between six and seven o'clock in the evening, while I was visiting with the widow Gautier on the rue des Belles-Filles, two peasants from the village of Laconnex approached me. One of them made a complaint against a certain Damoiselle accompanying them, who had left her daughter to be cared for by a wet nurse in Laconnex two years earlier, and had visited the girl and had given her some candy. They also claimed that she gave some candy to a five-year-old boy, son of the wet nurse, wife of the complainant. A moment after the children ate the candy, they were overtaken by convulsions. Seeing this, the Damoiselle, who had arrived accompanied by her cousin, and had been sitting at the table about to eat what the wet nurse had brought them, quickly got up.

Without any apparent concern for what was happening to her daughter and without waiting to find out what happened next, she immediately left the house with her cousin, claiming that her cousin was pressuring her to leave promptly so that he could return all the way to his home in Nyon that day.[1] She said that she was obliged to leave with him in order to avoid traveling unaccompanied and otherwise she would never have abandoned her daughter, who she did not think was sick enough to die, since she was as healthy as the other child. The two peasants declared that both children died less than two hours after eating the candy. The peasants had left the corpses of the children in Laconnex while they traveled to Geneva to report what had happened and receive orders about what to do next.

I then turned to the Damoiselle to ask what she had to say for herself. She protested that she knew nothing about the deaths of the children, except that which the peasants had told her. It is true that, seeing that her daughter had a distended belly and judging that she had worms, the deponent gave her the candy, which she said was safe, with no intention of harming her. At the same time, she also gave some candy to the other child and to the child's mother, both of whom took it and ate it; she and her cousin also had some. She believes that the worms caused the deaths of the two children since the wet nurse, the deponent, and her cousin ate the candy without anything happening to them.

I then asked the peasant, father of the dead boy, what he was hoping to achieve by making this complaint. He told me that he sought justice without wanting to become a civil plaintiff to the trial so as to avoid having anything to do with the investigation.[2] He was willing, if necessary, to be taken prisoner with the Damoiselle whom he accused of having caused the death of his child.

Next I asked the Damoiselle where she lived and she told me that she rented a room from the widow Fabri at the Place Bourg-de-Four and so we went there. In search of the truth, I asked the widow Fabri if the Damoiselle lived with her. She confirmed that the Damoiselle rented the upper bedroom. I then asked the widow if she would be willing to act as a defense witness for the Damoiselle, which she refused to do saying she did not wish to. I thought perhaps it was because the said Damoiselle [Jeanne Catherine] claimed to be a member of a very honorable family from Orbe in Switzerland.

---

[1] Nyon was a city located twenty-three kilometers northeast of Geneva in the Vaud region of Switzerland.

[2] Abraham Clerc could have instead initiated a civil suit against Jeanne Catherine in the hopes of receiving compensation for the death of his son.

Seeking to inform Monsieur the Mayor of this affair before taking the Damoiselle prisoner, I went to his home with the two peasants. There I explained the particulars of the case, which the peasants confirmed. The mayor ordered me to hold the Damoiselle in custody in her bedchamber and to inform the lieutenant of justice of the said events. I then made my way to the home of the widow Fabri, where I had left the Damoiselle in question, and required that she go up to her bedchamber. I then asked everyone else to leave us while I remained alone with the said Damoiselle to take her formal declaration, which is attached. Afterwards, I left Officer Canard to guard her while I went to the home of Monsieur the Lieutenant with the two peasants. There, having been apprised of the particulars and having listened to the peasants, he ordered me to take the said Damoiselle to the audience chamber in the city hall. Monsieur the Lieutenant summoned the councillors and required the Damoiselle to answer his questions fully, after which I was ordered to put her in a separate room in the prison. I also left the two peasants in prison at the request of the Damoiselle because she accused them of slander. I did all this and then wrote this report in Geneva on the 6th of May, 1686.

Humbert,
auditeur.

FOLIO 2

[May 6, 1686. Auditeur Humbert questioned Jeanne Catherine Thomasset at her home before her arrest. Jeanne Catherine reported that she had visited Laconnex earlier that day with Daniel de la Fléchère, her first cousin, member of a well-established noble family in the Vaud region of Switzerland. She admitted that her illegitimate daughter had been baptized by the Protestant minister Théodore Vautier, brother of her landlady in Geneva.]

Declaration made by Jeanne, daughter of François Thomasset, from Orbe in Switzerland, approximately twenty-six years old.

Testimony gathered by myself and recorded in my hand. Said and declared that she left Orbe last Sunday with one of her cousins, Daniel de la Fléchère of Nyon, to go to the village of Laconnex to see her daughter whom for the last two years she had left to be nursed by a peasant whose name she does not know. Once in Laconnex with her cousin, she gave some candy to her daughter and to the son of the peasant, after which, quite suddenly after eating it, the children began to vomit. The said Thomasset then made ready to leave because her cousin was pressuring her to go so that he could return to Nyon by nightfall. Asked whether she was single or married. She responded that she was unmarried and that she had conceived this child with a person from Geneva, whom she did not know, with whom she had relations at the Sovereign of France Inn and that she had given birth in Laconnex at the home of a peasant whose name she could not remember. Her daughter was baptized by Monsieur Vautier in the village of Cartigny.

Geneva, May 6, 1686

Humbert, *auditeur*

FOLIO 3

[May 6, 1686. First interrogation of Jeanne Catherine Thomasset in prison after her arrest.]

Testimony of Jeanne, daughter of Jean François Thomasset, tax assessor for the bailiff of Romainmôtier, approximately twenty-six years old.

How long has she lived in this city?
For two years.

Where does she live?
In the home of Damoiselle Fabri, the widow, who lives at the Place Bourg-de-Four.

Has she always lived with the said Damoiselle Fabri?
She has lived with Damoiselle Fabri but has also lived in the home of a bargeman named Gevray on the rue de Rhône where she and her brothers rented rooms and lived there together.

Where is she living now?
At the home of Damoiselle Fabri.

Did she not leave the city today?
She left at four thirty this morning, on foot, with her cousin named Daniel de la Fléchère. Together they went to Laconnex to the home of a woman named Jeanne Marie Bally[3] where a child of hers was being nursed.

How long has the said Bally been nursing her child?
For two years.

---

[3] Bally is not the correct family name of the wet nurse. Her name is actually Jeanne Marie Favre.

With whom did she become pregnant?
With a stranger whom she does not know.

Did her father and mother know she had this child?
No, there were certainly rumors, but they do not know.

Did her parents know about her pregnancy and the birth?
No.

Who was with her when she gave birth?
She gave birth at the home of Bally in Laconnex. No family members were
    present, only a woman from Massongy whom Bally had sent for.

Where was she living during her pregnancy?
She lived in her father's house until she went to Laconnex, about six weeks
    before the birth.

Where did she have relations with the stranger?
In this city, at the Sovereign of France Inn, where she lodged for seven or eight
    days.

Did the stranger know about the pregnancy?
Yes, but he only mocked her.

Where was the stranger staying?
She does not know, but she saw him every day at the inn.

How is it that she abandoned herself to this stranger without knowing him?
It resulted from the weakness of her spirit.

*How is it that, having declared her pregnancy to the stranger, she did not have
    him arrested in order to force him to marry her or to compel him to pay for the
    upkeep of the child?*
Because she feared her father.

How long did she spend time with the stranger?
She only spent seven or eight days with him.

*Why does she say that she only spent seven or eight days with him given that she
    already testified that he mocked her pregnancy?*
It is true that she only spent seven or eight days with him, but she heard tell that
    he ridiculed her for being pregnant.

<u>*Who directed her to the said Bally for the birth?*</u>[4]

---

[4] Text underlined here was either underlined in the original manuscript or marked with the
Latin words *nota bene* in the margins.

She went herself to find a place where she might give birth secretly.

Who accompanied her?
Those whom she met on the road.

This is not plausible since she would have had to tell everyone she met on the road that she was seeking a place to give birth.
She asked in two or three villages.

Which villages did she go to?
First, she went to Cologny and from there to a village near the mountain, and then to Laconnex.

Where was she living in Geneva before she went to Laconnex to give birth?
She lived in the Saint-Gervais neighborhood of Geneva with a poor widow whose name, and the name of her dead husband, she does not know.

Who sent her to the widow?
When she arrived by boat from Rolle[5] where she had gone after telling her father that she would be taking a look at some of his vineyards near the lake, she was taken to the said widow by an unknown person whom she had asked about finding a place to stay.

How long has Sieur de la Fléchère been in the city?
Since yesterday.

Where has he been staying?
He stayed in the home of Damoiselle Fabri, in the same room as herself. She slept in the bed and he slept on a mattress on the floor in the middle of the room.

Where is her cousin now?
He has left the city.

Did they not return together from Laconnex?
Yes.

Why did her cousin come to this city?
When the deponent was in Nyon yesterday, she asked her cousin to accompany her somewhere, without telling him where at first. Eventually she took him into her confidence, and she told him they would be going to Laconnex.

Who has been paying the wet nurse to take care of her child?
She paid for everything, with the exception of two months' pay.

---

[5] Rolle is a village located on the north shore of Lake Geneva in the Vaud region of Switzerland.

Where did she get the money to pay the said wet nurse?
She paid the wet nurse with anything she could find, even selling her necklaces.

Did no one give her money to pay for the wet nurse?
No. She did everything she could, even going so far as to borrow two *écus* from
   her cousin de la Fléchère, which she still has. She also borrowed twenty-
   seven *florins* one time and one *écu* another time from Damoiselle Gros, a
   trader who lives at the Place du Molard. To secure these loans, she pawned
   spoons that belong to [her cousin] Jean Pierre Christin from Orbe, who gave
   them to her to exchange because they were too small.

Has her child been baptized?
Yes. She was baptized in Cartigny by Monsieur Vautier. Her daughter's name is
   Jeanne and the husband of the wet nurse presented her at the baptism.

Why did she go to Laconnex this morning?
To pay the wet nurse the wages she owed her so that the wet nurse would not
   come to Geneva and expose the fact that the deponent is the mother of the
   said child.

Was the wet nurse in her house when she arrived?
No, but the mother of the wet nurse was there.

How did she enter the house?
She entered by the door facing the orchard, through which she had entered on
   previous visits, and not by the front door facing the path.

Had she gone to visit her daughter several times?
Yes, she has been three times.

With whom did she go?
The first time, she went alone. The second time she went with her brother, who
   is now dead. The third time with her cousin de la Fléchère.

Did her brother know that the child was hers?
Yes, because they lived together.

*When she entered the kitchen and did not find the wet nurse there, did she not
   send for her? Who was sent to find her?*
She thinks it was a child who went, but the wet nurse arrived almost
   immediately.

Did the mother of the wet nurse stay in the kitchen with them the entire time?
Yes.

Was her child in the crib when she entered the kitchen?
Yes, the mother of the wet nurse fetched her from the crib.

When she saw her child, did she not give her something to eat?
The child had soiled the bedclothes, so the mother of the wet nurse went to put a clean white undershirt on her, but the child did not want to be dressed. The deponent told the mother of the wet nurse that she could hold the child. At the same time as she dressed the child, the deponent gave her daughter a candy, which she took from a package she had in her pocket. She also gave candy to the wet nurse and her son.

What kind of candies were they?
There were long candies, round candies, and candied almonds.

Is it not true that as soon as her child and the child of the wet nurse ate the said sugar that they started to vomit?
Yes.

Is it not true that the said wet nurse, after having eaten the candy, also started to vomit?
No. She never vomited and she had no heartburn.

Did anyone else, besides the wet nurse and the two children, eat the candy?
Yes. She, her cousin de la Fléchère, the mother of the wet nurse, and another peasant, whom she thinks is the brother of the wet nurse, all ate the candy without anyone vomiting or having heartburn.

Were all the candies in the package eaten or were some left?
There were still thirty or so candies left in the package. The deponent left them with the wet nurse who can show you.

Where did she buy the candy?
She bought about an eighth of a pound of candy from Damoiselle Fabri.

What does she think might have caused the vomiting of the children?
She thinks that the sweetness of the candies stirred up the worms with which she thinks the children were infected. She had noticed her daughter's stomach was very distended even though the children had not yet eaten that day.

Is it not true that mixed among the candy there were other substances that could have caused the death of the children?
No, and God preserve us from such thoughts. She wishes that the corpses of the children be opened up to discover the cause of their death.

Did the children not die while she was there?
After having remained in Laconnex from about seven in the morning until about noon, she returned to Geneva. She saw her daughter and the child of the wet nurse put to bed and left them sleeping peacefully. She gave her

daughter a kiss before leaving and was accompanied by the wet nurse to the far end of the orchard. As she left, she told the wet nurse to send her husband to the city or to come herself to fetch some [medicinal] powders to give to her daughter.

What did the wet nurse say to her when the two children started vomiting?
The women said they thought that the sugar had aggravated the worms the children had. Acting on this belief, they fetched some milk and *orviétan* that they gave and applied to the children.

Seeing the children in such a state, how is it that she did not stay in Laconnex to see if this remedy was successful?
Her cousin wanted to leave for Geneva in order to be able to return to Nyon and she did not want him to leave so as to have his company [on the walk home]. Her cousin insisted that the children's condition was nothing serious, that the worms had risen to press against their hearts. Would it have pleased God, had she stayed, that this accident would not have happened.

Did she pay what she owed to the wet nurse today?
She only paid for a month since she did not have the money to pay the rest.

How is it that she did not give the two écus she had borrowed from her cousin to pay the wet nurse?
She only received the money from her cousin after returning to the city. She had told the wet nurse to come next Wednesday so that she could give her the money then.

If she left the children sleeping in Laconnex, how did she know they had died?
She only heard about their deaths from the husband of the wet nurse around seven in the evening when he ran into her in town. He told her to go speak with an *auditeur* since he was accusing her of having given something to his son that caused the death of both children.

Summoned to tell the truth. Is it not true that there was poison in the candy she gave to the children that might have caused their deaths?
She did not know there was anything wrong with the candies. After she bought them, she gave them, as is, to the children and to the others.

When did she buy the candies and from whom did she buy them?
She bought them yesterday evening directly from Damoiselle Fabri herself.

She must declare the name of the father of her child and declare what kind of promise he made to her in order for her to have abandoned herself to him and fornicated.

As she stated earlier, she does not know his name, but it is true that he gave her a gold chain that she sold to pay the wet nurse.

Does she not recognize that she committed a great sin, by committing fornication, by hiding her pregnancy, and by causing the death of two children?
She admits to having committed a grave sin by becoming pregnant, but, with regards to the deaths of the children, she is innocent.

To whom did she sell the gold chain and for how much?
She sold it to Sieur Archimbaud, she thinks, and she does not remember how much she received for it, but the chain weighed about thirty grams.

Did she give anything other than candy to the children?
No.

Given that she had only brought an eighth of a pound of candy for her child, how is it that she distributed it to peasants who have no habit of eating such things?
When one offers something to someone, one normally offers it to everyone present.

Had she brought candy the other times she had visited?
No, but she had brought some stewed vegetables.

Does she harbor suspicions against any person?
No.

This testimony was given in the presence of Monsieur the Lieutenant, Messieurs the *Auditeurs* Humbert, Turretini, and Du Puy. The said Thomasset did not wish to sign the document, saying that she did not have the strength.

Galiffe, clerk

FOLIO 4

[May 7, 1686. Deliberations of the Small Council. Throughout the trial, the Small Council regularly reviewed the proceedings and made executive decisions about how to move forward with the investigation. The Small Council also wrote to officials in other jurisdictions to ask for advice and to request the extradition of suspects. Each entry begins with a list of the councillors absent that day. The Small Council had twenty-five members.]

Friday, May 7, 1686.[6] Nobles Chabrey and Lect absent. Lieutenant of justice present.

---

[6] AEG RC 186, f. 134.

Jeanne Thomasset of Orbe. The lieutenant of justice reported having imprisoned the said Jeanne Thomasset, suspected of having poisoned her own illegitimate son [*sic*], conceived out of wedlock, that she was having nursed in Laconnex, and also of having poisoned the child of the wet nurse with candy. The husband of the wet nurse came forward as a denouncer in order that a criminal prosecution against her be undertaken. The lieutenant recommends that the corpses of the two children should be examined in order to discover the poison. The council then ordered the *châtelain* to accompany a physician and a surgeon to examine the corpses of the children. The Lord Lieutenant, responsible for drawing up the report, was urged, in doing so, to observe every necessary formality on behalf of the denouncer in order to discover the truth of this matter.

───────────────────── **FOLIO 5** ─────────────────────

[May 7, 1686. Interrogation in prison of Abraham Clerc, father of the dead boy. Abraham Clerc was imprisoned because Jeanne Catherine insisted that his accusations were slanderous. In his testimony, Abraham Clerc mentions that Gabriel and Gédéon Régis acted as intermediaries for Jeanne Catherine, making arrangements for the birth and paying the wet nurse on a regular basis. The Régis brothers were cousins of Jeanne Catherine.]

Testimony of Abraham, son of the late Étienne Clerc of Laconnex, approximately thirty-four years old.

Why is he a prisoner?
Because he declared that a Damoiselle, whose name he does not know, but
   who lives at the Place Bourg-de-Four in the house of the sister of Monsieur
   Vautier the minister, came to Laconnex yesterday morning to visit her child,
   whom she left to be nursed at the home of the deponent. Both her child
   and his own son, having been given something to eat, started to vomit and
   then fell into convulsions and started to foam at the mouth and died about
   two hours after the Damoiselle arrived. He came yesterday evening for this
   reason [to Geneva] to lodge a complaint with the magistrates.

Did he see the said Damoiselle give anything to the children?
No, but his mother and wife saw her give the children some candy.

*Did the said Damoiselle not give the said candy to the deponent or to other people
   in addition to the said children?*
She did not give any to him, and he does not know if she gave the candy to
   others because he was not at home at the time.

Did the children start to vomit shortly after the said Damoiselle arrived in Laconnex?

He cannot positively say, but the children started to vomit while the said Damoiselle and her cousin were starting to eat an omelet and eggs that his wife had made them. The said Damoiselle and her cousin then got up from the table without even having finished their eggs and left promptly, both of them saying that they were obliged to leave due to the illness of the father of the Monsieur. He did not hear them say this, because he was not in the house, but his wife and mother reported it to him.

Where was he at the time?

He was working, but when he returned to the house and saw the pitiful state that the children were in, vomiting and foaming at the mouth with their eyes closed, he ran to the village of Avully to fetch the surgeon. The surgeon returned with him and, seeing the pain the children were in, said that they had been poisoned and recommended coming to the city to tell the magistrates.

What did they do to try to care for the children?

They gave the children *orviétan* and several people came running to help and did everything imaginable to care for them.

Who brought the Damoiselle's child to be nursed in his home?

The Damoiselle herself with Monsieur Régis, who died some time ago. He paid the first months of service, then the said Damoiselle and her brother made subsequent payments so that they are only owed three or four months' pay.

Did the said Damoiselle ever send a powder to be given to her daughter to cure worms?

About a year ago, a girl was sent to give them something wrapped in a paper with instructions to give it to the said child, but since they did not know the said girl and did not want to give anything to the child without explicit permission, they kept the powder instead and returned it to Monsieur Régis who said he would have it tested by an apothecary.

Does he not know the name of the father of the child?

No. The said Damoiselle did not even want to admit his name to the minister, Monsieur Vautier.

Has the said Damoiselle often visited her daughter and has the Monsieur who accompanied her yesterday ever visited before?

The said Damoiselle has visited three or four times since the child was left with them, but the said Monsieur he had never seen before.

How old were the children and were they in good health?
His son was five years old and the daughter of the said Damoiselle was two, and
  they were perfectly well.

When that girl brought something as a remedy for worms, was the girl sick?
No, the said child was well.

Who was in the house when the said Damoiselle gave candy to the children?
His mother, his wife and his brother-in-law named Pierre Favre of Avully.

*Had the children not had convulsions on other occasions and were they not
  accustomed to vomiting?*
No, he had never seen either of them sick.

*The other times when the said Damoiselle visited her daughter, did she not also
  give candy to her?*
No, she never brought anything or gave anything to the children, at least to his
  knowledge.

Did they ever complain to the said Damoiselle that her daughter had worms?
No, he never noticed that she had them or was sick in any way.

Summoned to tell the truth.
Has done so.
Repeated, read aloud, and he affirmed his testimony. He did not sign because he
  does not know how.

Humbert, auditeur
Du Puy, auditeur

*When he came to the city last night, did he not see the said Damoiselle and speak
  with her?*
When he came to the city to make his complaint, he ran after the said
  Damoiselle who pretended not to see him. He seized her dress and told her
  to come with him to speak with an *auditeur* in order to explain what she had
  given to the children who were dead. At first, she said that she would return
  with him to Laconnex and refused to go to the *auditeur*. She begged him not
  to say a word and wanted to bring him into the house where she lived, which
  he refused to do. He was determined not to leave her side until she spoke
  with *Auditeur* Sieur Humbert.

Humbert, Du Puy, auditeurs

───────────────── **FOLIO 6** ─────────────────

[May 7, 1686. Interrogation in prison of Pierre Quiby, uncle of Abraham Clerc, great-uncle of the dead boy. He had accompanied his nephew to Geneva to make the accusation against Jeanne Catherine.]

Testimony of Pierre, son of the late Pierre Quiby of Laconnex, about fifty years old.

> *Why is he a prisoner?*
> Because he declared that a Damoiselle, whose name he does not know but who lives with the widow Fabri at the Place Bourg-de-Four, came yesterday morning to Laconnex to visit her child, who was being nursed at the home of his nephew Abraham Clerc. Once the Damoiselle gave the children something to eat, a moment later both of them began to vomit and then fell into convulsions and died two hours later.
>
> *Was the said Damoiselle alone?*
> She brought a man with her whom she said was a cousin.
>
> *Who was in the Clerc house when the said Damoiselle arrived?*
> No one except the mother of Abraham Clerc. The said Damoiselle ordered her to go and fetch the wet nurse, her daughter-in-law, and she went to do so, leaving the said Damoiselle with her cousin alone with the children.
>
> *Did he see the said Damoiselle give the children something to eat?*
> No, but the wet nurse told many other people that the said Damoiselle gave them candy, which the said Damoiselle has admitted to having done, saying that it was a powder to cure worms.
>
> *Does he know whether anyone besides the wet nurse saw the said Damoiselle give anything else to the children?*
> No.
>
> *How old were the children and were they healthy?*
> The daughter of the said Damoiselle was about two years old and the son of the wet nurse was five and both were in good health.
>
> *Who paid for the said girl to be nursed?*
> At first, the Régis brothers paid, but about a year ago the said Damoiselle sent something wrapped in paper with instructions to give it to her child to cure her of worms. The wet nurse did not want to give [the substance] to the child, so she gave the paper and all that was in it to the Messieurs Régis and since then they have not wanted to interfere with the child.

Did the said Damoiselle give birth in Laconnex?
Yes, at the home of Thivent Giron.

*Did the children start to vomit soon after the said Damoiselle arrived in
   Laconnex?*
When the wet nurse first arrived, she made them an omelet and started to cook
   some fresh eggs. The said Damoiselle and the said cousin sat at the table to
   eat, but when they saw the children starting to vomit, both of them, at the
   same time, changed color. The said Damoiselle and her cousin got up from
   the table right away, even though they had barely started eating, and quickly
   left.

*Who was present when this happened and how did they explain why they were
   leaving so hastily?*
As far as he knows, only the wet nurse, her brother, and her mother-in-law were
   in the house. The said cousin of the said Damoiselle claimed that they had to
   leave immediately because his father was very ill.

Did the children continue to vomit after the said Damoiselle left?
Their pain and distress increased, with more and more grinding of teeth and
   grimaces. The wet nurse called several people who did all they could to
   soothe them, but it was useless because they died soon afterwards, both of
   them at the same time.

*Is it possible that they experienced some very powerful convulsions but that they
   did not die? Perhaps people arrived at the house and gave their opinions a little
   too quickly?*
They definitely died. He asked several people who were present, in particular a
   surgeon who lives in Avully who the husband of the wet nurse brought to the
   house. Seeing the children, he said that he thought they had been poisoned
   and that they had waited too long to fetch him.

*Had the children not had convulsions on other occasions and did they not
   sometimes vomit?*
No, both of the children were perfectly well.

*Does he know whether the said Damoiselle remained in the village of Laconnex
   once she left the home of the wet nurse?*
No, on the contrary, his son saw both her and the man who had come with her
   leaving quickly for the city.

*When he and the said Clerc his nephew arrived in the city yesterday evening did
   they not go to speak with the said Damoiselle?*

Yes, when his nephew found her near the Boulevard Saint-Antoine,[7] he grabbed her dress and told her to come speak with an *auditeur* about what she had given the two children to eat that had killed them. The said Damoiselle said to them several times in a desperate voice to be quiet, to stop talking, to say nothing more, and that she would go with them immediately to see the children.

Does he know whether the said Damoiselle gave candy to people other than the children?
No.

Did the said Damoiselle visit her daughter often and had her cousin accompanied her before?
The cousin had never visited before yesterday, but the said Damoiselle had visited three or four times since she gave birth.

Summoned to tell the truth.
Has done so.
Repeated, read aloud, and he affirmed his testimony. He did not sign because he does not know how.

Humbert and Du Puy, auditeurs

FOLIO 7

[May 7, 1686. Declaration of Jeanne Vautier, the widow Fabri, Jeanne Catherine's landlady, taken by Auditeur Jean Pierre Bagueret. Bagueret was a silk manufacturer and merchant and had just recently become a public investigator. It is very likely that Jeanne Vautier and Jean Pierre Bagueret, who were about the same age, would have already known each other.]

Declaration of Damoiselle Jeanne Vautier, widow of the late Noble Urbain Fabri, approximately sixty years old, swears the oath.

Declared and testified that she knows [blank space] Thomasset because about seven months ago she started living in her house. The deponent provided furniture for the bedchamber where Thomasset lived for approximately six months consecutively. Then, after her brother died, the said Thomasset left for one month to go to the Vaud region. Thomasset returned [to Geneva from the Vaud] Wednesday evening of this week, accompanied

---

[7] The Boulevard Saint-Antoine is located near the city ramparts and just a few minutes' walk from the Place Bourg-de-Four where Jeanne Catherine lived.

by a forty-year-old man whom the Damoiselle believes is a relative and has sometimes visited Thomasset. She does not know whether the said man slept in the bedchamber of Thomasset because the said chamber is specially for Thomasset and is above the chamber of the deponent. Wednesday about seven o'clock in the evening Thomasset bought an eighth of a pound of candy from the deponent, which she took from the same box that she gave to Monsieur Bagueret, *auditeur*. Thomasset did not tell the deponent what she intended to do with the candy and the deponent did not see the said Thomasset again that night or the next day before two in the afternoon when she entered the shop to take some oil, having bought a salad from a shop in the neighborhood, and asked for some wine. She gave her wine from a jug and guessed that Thomasset had company since she did not usually ask for provisions between meals. After that, around five o'clock in the afternoon, having heard the rumor that Thomasset had been accused of a crime, the deponent, trembling with horror at the said crime, went to the bedchamber of Thomasset to ask her whether she had gone to Laconnex. Thomasset at first denied it, but, when asked a second time, she admitted to having gone. After that, the deponent told her what was being said about her. Thomasset seemed very surprised and shocked to hear the report, saying that people were speaking ill of her, that she was not the sort of girl who would do that, and that she needed to speak to those who were saying these things. At which point, Thomasset left the house, but returned not long after led by a peasant to Monsieur Humbert *auditeur* and his officers, who spoke to her [Jeanne Catherine] soon afterwards and took her to the city hall, which is all that the deponent knows.

The declaration was read aloud, the witness confirmed her testimony, and signed.

Jane Vatier [*sic*]
Bagueret, *auditeur*

FOLIO 8

[*May 7/17, 1686.*[8] *Evidence collected by Marc Sarasin, châtelain, judicial official in charge of investigating crime in the village of Laconnex. Genevan officials traveled to Laconnex to collect witness testimony from the villagers.*

---

[8] During the seventeenth century, the official calendar of Geneva was the Julian calendar. Since 1582, however, most Catholic states in Europe had adopted the new Gregorian calendar. A handful of the documents in the trial dossier generated by private individuals nevertheless

Each villager testified privately and under oath in the presence of the châtelain and the clerk François Joly who transcribed their testimony.]

Information gathered in Laconnex, in the home of Abraham Clerc the younger, by the named Marc Sarasin, *châtelain* for the territory of St. Victor, on behalf of our magnificent and very honorable Lords of Geneva, based on the signed order issued by our magnificent and very honorable Lord regarding the sudden death of both the son of the said Clerc and the child whom the wife of the said Clerc was nursing. Arrived in Laconnex expediently on horseback, accompanied by François Joly, clerk of St. Victor. Returned to Geneva on horseback.

————

First, honorable Jeanne Marie, daughter of honorable Louis Favre of Avully, wife of honorable Abraham Clerc of Laconnex, laborer, about thirty-two years of age. Has taken the oath to tell the truth.

Declared and testified that, two years earlier, in April 1684, a Damoiselle living in Laconnex at the time gave birth to a girl in the home of Thivent Giron in the presence of the deponent. The child was presented for baptism in the church in Cartigny by her husband Abraham Clerc and was given to her to nurse by Sieur Gabriel Régis arranged to provide food for the child. She received her monthly wages from him and from time to time from the said Damoiselle. She does not know the name of the said Damoiselle, though she did hear the late Sieur Régis and his brother Sieur Gédéon Régis mention that her name was Thomasset when they came to pay her from time to time. The deponent declared that she does not know the name of the father of the child since the said Damoiselle never declared it even though she came to visit her child three different times. One time, the said Thomasset came dressed as a servant accompanied by another Damoiselle whom the deponent did not know but whom the said Thomasset referred to as her cousin. Adding, about a year ago, the said Thomasset sent by means of a Savoyard girl a twist of paper containing two tablets and some powder. When asked who brought her the tablets and powder, the deponent responded that it was a servant girl, whose name she did not know and had no acquaintance with. When she gave her the twist of paper, the said

employed the new Gregorian dating system. This discrepancy is noted in the Small Council records by recording both dates: the date before the slash is the date according to the Julian calendar and the date after the slash indicates the Gregorian calculation.

servant told the deponent to give the tablets and powder to the child she
was nursing when the moon was waning. The deponent did not want to
do so because she did not know the servant nor the nature of the powder.
Also because the child did not seem ill, she gave the tablets and powder to
Sieur Gédéon Régis whom she encountered in Geneva at Plainpalais without knowing what he did with them.

Also testified that yesterday around eight in the morning, while she
was at the fountain, her mother came to tell her to return to the house
immediately. When she arrived home, she found the said Thomasset with
a stranger, whom she did not know but whom Thomasset treated like a
cousin. The deponent asked the said Thomasset whether she thought that
her child was in good health, and she answered yes, and the deponent then
noticed that the child had a candy in her hand. A moment later, the said
Thomasset took more candy from her pocket, which she put on the table,
the remainders of which the deponent has given to us, and told the deponent to have some. And the Damoiselle and her cousin ate some in order to
encourage them to do so because the deponent hesitated. She did not notice
whether the said Thomasset gave a different candy to the two children, who
are now dead, than the type she had given to everyone else. The deponent
surmises that the said Thomasset gave the children a powder when she was
alone in the house with the said stranger while the deponent's mother-in-
law came to fetch her at the fountain. The deponent does not remember
whether she ate any of the candy herself.

Also declares that, a moment later, Thomasset's child and her own
son began to vomit and changed color in such a way that they almost lost
consciousness. At this point, Thomasset said that their sickness was the
result of the sugar, which irritated them because they were infected with
worms and that it was necessary to give them *orviétan*, which the deponent
promptly did. She heard the said Thomasset say that she wished she had
handed over an *écu* and had not given something to the children, without
specifying what it was. When the *orviétan* did not work, and, on the contrary, the children worsened minute to minute, the said stranger said to the
said Thomasset that he wanted to leave because his father was indisposed.
Thomasset replied that she wanted to wait some time in order to learn more
about the state of the said children. Nevertheless, the said Thomasset did
decide, without waiting much longer, to leave between nine and ten o'clock
in the morning. When she left, she said to the deponent that she needed to
come to Geneva to fetch a powder. The said stranger added that there was
no need to come before next Wednesday because the moon would be at the
right stage then to give it to the children. Declared that the said Thomasset
gave her an *écu* as a deposit toward what she still owed her for taking care of

her child and advised her to take good care, saying this as she left. Testifying in addition that her son died between two and three in the afternoon and that the daughter of the said Thomasset died shortly afterwards. The children were not sick before they saw the said Thomasset but were in good health and she does not know anything else other than the fact that the said Thomasset had a brother who died in Geneva of worms and that the physicians had not been able to diagnose his illness before he died.

The testimony was read aloud, the witness confirmed her testimony, and did not sign because she cannot write.

Sarasin

Joly, clerk

————

Honorable Louise, daughter of the late Daniel Ducré, widow of honorable Étienne Clerc, laborer of Laconnex, about sixty years old, has taken the oath as did the last witness.

Testified that while living with Abraham Clerc her son, a Damoiselle, whose name she did not know, even though she had seen her several times at her son's house, visited her own child, who was being nursed by the wife of Abraham Clerc. Yesterday morning, about eight o'clock, the said Damoiselle arrived with a man, whom she did not know, and entered the house of said Clerc, in which she, the deponent, was alone, to ask her where the wet nurse was. The deponent replied that she was at the fountain washing the children's clothes. At that moment, the said Damoiselle asked whether her daughter was awake, which she was not, so the deponent went to get the daughter of the said Damoiselle who is called Thomasset and also the child of her son. Once they were both up and dressed, the deponent noticed the said Thomasset giving both of them candy. The said Damoiselle also gave the deponent some candy, which she ate without feeling unwell afterwards. Then the said Thomasset asked her to bring her a cup, which the deponent did immediately, and also asked her for some wine, to which the deponent replied that there was wine in the jug. Just then, the said Damoiselle ordered the deponent to go and find the wet nurse, which she did right away, leaving the said Thomasset and the stranger alone in the said house with the children without having noticed what the said Thomasset did with the cup nor having been told what she planned to do with it. Adding that when she returned from the fountain, the deponent found the wife of Abraham Clerc, the said Thomasset, and the stranger with the children in the house. A moment later, the two children started to vomit with such force that her daughter-in-law called out and said that the children would surely die, at which point the said Thomasset said that she should not be concerned, that it was just the effect of the sugar that she had given them because of the worms they had inside them that were rising to their hearts. She also said that the sugar could not have harmed the children since the said Damoiselle, the stranger, and the deponent had also eaten some, that it was the same sugar. The deponent did not know whether the said Damoiselle had given something to drink to the children while she left the house to get her daughter-in-law. Regardless, the children continued to vomit and were dying moment by moment so the said Thomasset said that they needed to give them some *orviétan*, which they did, but to no avail because the children experienced no relief at all. Her daughter-in-law was distraught to see the children so sick, and the said Thomasset told them that she had a brother who had died some time ago in Geneva of worms and that the physicians who treated him could not diagnose his illness. The deponent added that the stranger, whom the said Thomasset called cousin, said to Thomasset that he needed to leave promptly because his father was grievously ill and told her to return to Geneva with him. The said Thomasset replied that she very much wanted to wait until the children improved from the unknown illness. But she did leave with the stranger soon afterwards, around nine or ten o'clock in the morning, having told the wet nurse to come to Geneva to buy some powder for the worms that were giving the children so much trouble. Declaring as well that the child of the said Abraham Clerc died between two and three o'clock in the afternoon after much suffering, and that the daughter of the said Thomasset died a moment later. Testified that the children were well and showed no sign of illness before the arrival of Thomasset and knows nothing more.

Repeated and read aloud, the witness confirmed her testimony, and did not sign.

Sarasin
Joly, clerk

———

Honorable Pierre, son of honorable Louis Favre, laborer in Avully, about thirty-four years old, took the oath in the same way as previous witnesses.

Testified that yesterday about eight o'clock in the morning when he arrived in Laconnex at the home of his brother-in-law Abraham Clerc, he found there the said Damoiselle stranger accompanied by a man, both of whom he did not know, though he learned at that moment that she was the mother of the girl that the wife of Abraham Clerc was nursing. They were all sitting at the table eating together and he joined them for a drink. The deponent declared that, a moment later, the daughter of the said Damoi-selle started to vomit, at which the said Damoiselle said that one need not worry, that it was probably the candy that she had given her, that had not gone down well because of the worms that she had. A moment later, the same illness struck the child of Abraham Clerc, which caused the said Damoiselle to tell the wet nurse that they needed to give the children *orvié-tan* immediately and to go into the garden to find some garlic with which to rub their necks, which was done right away. The deponent then heard the said Damoiselle say that she did not want to leave without knowing how the children were doing, that if she had not herself eaten some candy too she would think that the sweets were the cause of the children's illness. He then testified that he himself had eaten a sweet without any ill effect, but that he had not seen what the children had eaten nor what she had given them. Declared not to know what sickness led to their death. He left the house before the said Damoiselle and the stranger. Does not know anything further.

Repeated, read aloud, witness confirmed testimony, did not sign.

Sarasin
Joly, clerk

———

Honorable Gilbert, son of the late honorable Gabriel Deromieux of Vivarez, master apothecary living in Avully, about thirty-two years of age, taken the oath like the others.

Testified that yesterday, about two o'clock in the afternoon, when he was in Avully, the said Abraham Clerc the younger of Laconnex came to find him and asked him to come immediately to his house in Laconnex to tend to two children who were very ill and whom he thought had been poisoned by the mother of the girl that his wife was nursing. The deponent mounted a horse and arrived promptly in Laconnex at the house of Abraham Clerc. Once he arrived, they showed him the children, and, after having exam-ined them, he concluded that their sickness was incurable and that they would soon die. Nevertheless, he set himself the task of preparing some-thing to relieve their immediate suffering. While he was doing so, they brought the son of Abraham Clerc to him: he had already died and given up his soul. The deponent continued to prepare a remedy that would have been useful to the girl, who had the same sickness, but she too rendered her spirit a moment after that of the son of Abraham Clerc without his having needed to give them any medication. He sincerely believes, based on his knowledge, that the children were poisoned, both because he noticed that their tongues were black and that the matter that they vomited was also black and burnt. The deponent does not know who committed this crime though he heard from those at the home of Abraham Clerc that it was the mother of the said girl, as he has already stated. He did not witness anything further, knows nothing else, and said no more.

Repeated, read aloud, witness confirmed testimony, and signed Deromieux.

Sarasin
Joly, clerk

———

Honorable Jacquema, daughter of the late Pierre Couly, widow of honorable Pierre Mery, laborer of Laconnex, about seventy years of age, taken the same oath as the others.

She testified that, about two years ago, the wife of Thivent Giron of Laconnex came by [in order to ask her] to come to her home to help a Damoiselle, whom no one knew, give birth. The deponent immediately went and found the said Damoiselle lying in the Giron family bed. A moment later, the Damoiselle rose from the bed and started to walk around to encourage the birth. The birth occurred moments later and the witness caught the child, which she affirms was alive. She does not know the name of the father nor the name of the mother because the said Damoiselle did not wish to declare it, despite the deponent's insistence that she do so. Adding that she heard the said Damoiselle ask the good Lord to take her daughter after she was baptized. The day after the birth, the baby was taken to Cartigny to be baptized, but the honorable Théodore Vautier expressed some doubts about doing so because he had not been told whom the baby belonged to. The said Damoiselle went to him and made him understand that he should not cause her pain or pressure her to reveal the name of the father because she does not have the right nor the desire to name him. The said child was then put to nurse at the home of Abraham Clerc the younger in Laconnex. The deponent declared that yesterday, about three in the afternoon, while at home, her daughter-in-law came to tell her that the child of Abraham Clerc and the daughter of the said Damoiselle were both dead, which caused the deponent to quickly go to them. Once there, she noticed that they were both in agony and died moments later. Denied knowing what sickness could have killed them so suddenly, because the day before she had seen both of them in good health, unaffected by any illness. Does not know anything more.

Repeated, read aloud, witness confirmed testimony, and did not sign.

Sarasin

Joly, clerk

———

Honorable Claudine, daughter of Claude Girard, wife of Étienne Giron, laborer of Laconnex, about fifty-two years old, taken the oath like the others.

Testified that about two years ago the late Gabriel Régis brought to her home a Damoiselle who was pregnant and whose first name was Beatrix and the deponent does not know if she has a family name. She gave birth to a daughter about three weeks later in the home of the deponent. The baby was birthed by Jacquema Mery and the next day was baptized in the church of Cartigny, presented for baptism by Abraham Clerc the younger. The deponent declared not to have discovered the name of the father of the said child even though she did her best to find out from the said Damoiselle. It was principally for this reason that Minister Vautier expressed some doubts about baptizing the child since he did not know whom she belonged to. Declaring as well that the said Damoiselle lived in her home for about three weeks after the birth and that she has not seen her since then because the said Damoiselle has been avoiding her, even though she has returned to the home of the said Clerc to visit her daughter several times. The deponent does not know what caused the death of the child of Abraham Clerc and the daughter of the said Damoiselle, but can say that last Wednesday she saw the two children about the village and they seemed well. Does not know anything else.

Repeated, read aloud, witness confirmed testimony, and did not sign.

Sarasin

Joly, clerk

——————————————— FOLIO 9 ———————————————

[May 7/17, 1686. Report of Marc Sarasin, châtelain of the territory of St. Victor where Laconnex was located. Sarasin makes reference to the testimony of two university-trained physicians Daniel Le Clerc and Dominique Beddevole, both of whom were citizens of Geneva. He also refers to the testimony of two surgeons, Étienne Dentand and Étienne Demonthoux, also citizens of Geneva.]

We the undersigned, judge of the territory of St. Victor for our magnificent and very honorable Lords of Geneva, certify that we were ordered to visit the village of Laconnex, in the territory of St. Victor, accompanied by respected Étienne [*sic*] Le Clerc, Dominique Beddevole, physicians, by Messieurs Étienne Dentand and Étienne Demonthoux, master surgeons, and by François Joly, our clerk, to investigate the deaths of two children that occurred the day before in the home of Abraham Clerc. Arriving about nine or ten in the morning, we found the children in the home of the honorable Abraham Clerc extended on the table, wrapped in cloth, and learned that one of them, who was about five years old, belonged to the said Abraham Clerc, and that the other, about two years of age, belonged to a foreigner named Thomasset. In order to discover the cause of their sudden and extraordinary deaths, we asked the respected Le Clerc and Beddevole and Messieurs Dentand and Demonthoux to swear faithfully to examine the children, and to proceed in this examination without any passion or hate or favor. Having received their oaths, Sieurs Dentand and Demonthoux cut open the children, by our order and in our presence. The children were then examined and observed by the respected Le Clerc and Beddevole together with the named surgeons. They all came to the same conclusion that the children had been poisoned, as demonstrated by the results of their report of May 8th, signed by all of them. After this, we proceeded to question the named witnesses under oath in the attached document. These depositions, taken together, all confirmed that the said Thomasset, accompanied by a stranger, arrived the day before about eight or nine in the morning in Laconnex at the home of the said Abraham Clerc. About half an hour after her arrival, the said children were distressed by great vomiting and weakness of the limbs, which the said witnesses attributed to the said Thomasset having given the children some candy, because beforehand they seemed perfectly well. And that the said Thomasset, instead of waiting and remaining with her child in order to offer her comfort, left promptly with the stranger under the pretext that his father was grievously ill. The children died later that day, about three in the afternoon. All of this information is contained in the attached depositions, and we have expedited our final report, written in Laconnex on the 17th of May, 1686.

Sarasin

FOLIO 10

[May 7/17, 1686. Autopsy report of the physicians Le Clerc and Beddevole and the surgeons Dentand and Demonthoux.]

We the undersigned physicians and master surgeons certify and attest in the following document the oath we took before Monsieur the judge of St. Victor, in the village of Laconnex, where we had been transported by the orders of our very honorable Lords, this day the 17th of May in order to conduct an autopsy of two corpses in the house of Abraham Clerc.

We found various parts of the exterior of the girl to be purple and black, for example the tops of the shoulders, the ears, all along the neck and the back, the eyelids, to the right of the stomach, as well as the fingernails and toenails. The lower abdomen was distended, the tongue black on top but otherwise white and dried out as if it had been cooked, similarly the gums and the inside of the lips, and all the flesh of the body soft. Once we opened the body, we next observed that the liver was black in several places, particularly on the right side; the gall bladder was filled with a green bile; and the omentum[9] shrunken. Having opened the ventricle, it was filled with a black sack, at the bottom of which we felt a material that was granular, heavy, rough to the touch, and a pale yellow in color. The said ventricle was abraided and showed various signs of inflammation, particularly toward the superior orifice. All along the intestines were also black and red in places and especially the small intestines of the colon were also very inflamed and filled with worms of different sizes, as many as sixty in total. Finally, the blood was very black and entirely degraded, in the ears and the ventricles of the heart, as well as elsewhere.

Having then opened the corpse of the son of Abraham Clerc, about five years old, we found the abdomen swollen, the flesh to be fairly soft, the tongue dried out, and even the gums ulcerated, with blackness on the back, the ears, and the nails. The omentum was similarly shrunken. The liver was blackened on the right side. There was even a small ulceration in the hollow about the size of a lentil, toward the small lobe, which was also inflamed. The gall bladder was black in several spots and contained viscous dark yellow bile. The stomach was similarly filled with a black sack containing small yellow grains and to the touch it seemed in greater quantity than in the girl. Also the stomach was more damaged, the ulcerations were more visible and profound, both toward the superior orifice and a bit lower toward the bottom, at the *tunique interieure*,[10] a degradation the size of a coin was found. Both the large and small intestines showed various

---

[9] The greater omentum is a large apron-like fold of membrane that hangs down from the stomach.

[10] The *tunique interieure* was a Galenic term to describe a membrane near the base of the esophagus, but here may make reference to another part of the digestive system. Galen was a Greek physician of the second century CE.

signs of inflammation and degradation, and were encased by groups of very black and swollen veins. Another remarkable observation was that the valve of the colon was all red at the extremity. The glands attached to the fold of the peritoneum that connects to the posterior intestinal wall and those along the intestines were very swollen, as in the girl, and there were as many or more worms. The blood was similarly degraded and black. The lung was black on the right side; the spleen had some red spots. With regards to the rest of the middle and lower abdomen, they were both in their natural state.

We then withdrew to confer together on all that we had observed, and concluded unanimously that the two children had been poisoned, which would explain the blackness, inflammation, ulceration of different parts, especially the stomach and the intestines, the black liquid, and the heavy granular materials found in the stomach, which we have set aside for further examination, and other signs of poison that we have reported here. It is not possible that the worms that we found caused the said deaths. Further clarification can be found in the symptoms that developed during the sickness of the children. We were told that the children vomited with great violence, were greatly altered, were lethargic, their extremities were very cold etc. Further, the resemblance of the two deaths to one another and the fact that the children died on the same day and almost the same hour, the truth of which the Lords of justice will further investigate specifically. Such is our report, in witness thereof, we have all signed. Completed at Laconnex the 17th of May, 1686.

Le Clerc, physician; Beddevole, physician.
Étienne Demonthoux, master surgeon.
Étienne Dentand the Elder, master surgeon.

FOLIO 11

[May 7, 1686. Second interrogation of Jeanne Catherine Thomasset.]

Testimony of Jeanne Catherine Thomasset, about twenty-six years old, from Agiez near Orbe.

Who got her pregnant before she went to Laconnex?
She cannot say because she does not know him.

Where did she have relations with him?
In Geneva, in her room at the Sovereign of France Inn.

Did the stranger stay with her there?

She does not know where he was staying.

Did she ever eat with him in the inn?
She ate with him there once or twice.

How did she get to know the said stranger?
It was a chance encounter.

How is it that she abandoned herself to an unknown person?
It was weakness.

Summoned to tell the truth. Is it not true that one of her family members got her
pregnant?
She has told the truth. She is miserable to have abandoned herself to this
stranger, but it is nevertheless the truth.

Did she abandon herself to the stranger because he made her some sort of promise
or payment?
He kept promising that he would marry her, which he never did, but he did give
her a gold chain.

When did he give her the gold chain?
In order to win her over before they had relations.

How long ago was it that she received the gold chain?
Her child is two and a quarter years old, so it would have been three years ago.

Had she been in the city long?
It was several days after she started staying at the Sovereign of France Inn.

Why had she come to Geneva?
She had come to buy some toiletries.

Did she come to the city alone?
She arrived in Geneva with the people she had met along the way, from Agiez,
a village near Orbe, all the way to Nyon, and from Nyon to here, but none of
them were from her home town or were people she knew.

Did her father and mother know about her departure? How is it that they allowed
her to travel all alone?
Her parents definitely knew, but they indulged her by allowing her to come here
all by herself.

Had she always lived at home before she came to stay at the Sovereign of France
Inn?
No, she has lived in various places in the Vaud region at the homes of relatives.

Did she tell her parents that she was coming to Geneva?

Yes.

What kind of a gold chain did the said stranger give her?
A chain, with some of the links textured and others smooth. The strand was about the thickness of a needle and went around her neck twice.

Does she still have the chain?
No, she sold it at a loss to Sieur Archimbaud.

How much did she sell it for?
She does not remember and did not think they would ask her that.

How long ago was it that she sold it?
She has no clear memory of it, but she thinks that it was a year, or a year and a half ago.

How much did it weigh?
She has no memory of the weight, just as she does not remember when she sold it or how much she received for it.

How long did she know the said stranger with whom she had relations?
She does not know what to say, but perhaps six months. He spent all of the winter in Geneva.

Did the said stranger have relations with her shortly after he met her?
He made several attempts to be intimate with her, and after fifteen days she abandoned herself to him.

Did she ever try to find out where the stranger was from?
Yes, but she only asked him about it.

Did he tell her where he was from?
Yes, but she does not recall anymore.

Did she not tell him that he was responsible for her pregnancy?
She could not tell him during the short time he stayed in Geneva.

<u>*Did she not let him know that she was pregnant?*</u>
<u>She did let him know, but he was cruel enough not to make good on it.</u>

What country and what nation was the stranger from and what was his profession?
She did not ask and could not say what his profession was since she never noticed whether he wore a sword.

Where did she live after she left the Sovereign of France Inn?
She returned home.

*When she returned home, did she tell her father or mother or other relatives about
her pregnancy?*
No, she told no one.

Did she not tell any relatives or friends about the pregnancy?
No, she hid the information from everyone.

Did she remain at home until she gave birth?
No, she left home six weeks before she gave birth.

Where did she go?
She went with a valet, on horseback, to the village of Tartegnin, near Lake
Geneva where her father owns some vineyards.

Did she stay there long?
Three or four days.

Did she go there by choice or because her father and mother ordered her to?
She arrived during the season when the grape vines are burned to fertilize the soil
and she used this as a pretext to ask permission from her father and mother to
go there. After that, she traveled along the lake all alone to reach Geneva.

With whom did she stay when she arrived in Geneva?
She stayed with a widow in the Saint-Gervais neighborhood, though she does
not know her name or the name of her former husband. She stayed there
four or five days and from there went to Cologny to stay in the home of
Monsieur de Chasteauvieux for about fifteen days during which time she had
a girl with her named Roze given to her by a person whose name she does
not recall. From Cologny, she went to a village near the mountain. And from
there to Laconnex where she gave birth.

Where did she give birth at Laconnex?
At the home of a woman named Jeanne Marie Clerc or Bally.

Who was present for the birth?
The woman named Clerc, her mother, and a woman from Massongy.

Did she have the child baptized?
Yes, the baptism took place in Cartigny and the child was given the name
Jeanne.

How long did she stay in Laconnex?
She remained there for about a month.

*During this entire time, did she not write to her father and mother to give them
her news?*

No, and they were so distressed that they sent Sieur Margel, her brother-in-law, to search for her in Thonon and Evian and in other places in Savoy. Finally he found her in Laconnex, but she hid and did not want to see him since she had just recently given birth. When she did see him, she told him that she had been sick without declaring that she had had a child, having hidden the child from him.

Did Sieur Margel not give her money to pay for her medical expenses?
No. It is true that the said Margel did ask her if she needed anything. She said she needed nothing and he then left.

Where did she go after she recovered from the birth and left Laconnex?
She came here where she stayed for seven or eight days with Damoiselle Blandin in the Saint-Gervais neighborhood.

Who paid for the birth?
She paid as she had enough money to do so.

Where did she stay after she left the home of Damoiselle Blandin?
She returned home to her parents.

Did her parents not express irritation that she had been gone for so long?
When they first saw her, they asked if she had recovered from her illness. Later they did express irritation with her, but she debased herself, acting submissive, and never told them that she had had a child, even though they pressured her to declare it.

Who took responsibility for paying the monthly fee to the wet nurse while she was absent?
She provided money two or three months in advance.

Is it not true that the late Sieur Régis paid the wet nurse for her?
Yes.

Is it not true that old Sieur Régis accompanied her when she left the child with the wet nurse?
Yes.

Is it not true that Sieur Gédéon Régis also paid the monthly fee to the wet nurse?
She thinks he paid one month's worth.

What interest did Messieurs Régis have in this affair?
It is because they are family members.

Where did she stay in Geneva the first time she left her parents' home after giving birth?

She rented rooms with her two brothers at the home of Qeurin on the rue de Rhône where she lived for thirteen months with her two brothers and with the consent of her father. After that and ever since, she lodged at the home of Mademoiselle Fabri, with the exception of a three-week absence.

During those weeks was she staying at her father's?
Yes. She left her father's home Sunday after church services and went to Nyon. She stayed there until Wednesday when she and her cousin Daniel de la Fléchère traveled together to Geneva. They stayed with the said Damoiselle Fabri at the Place Bourg-de-Four where her cousin had supper with her and slept in the same room as herself on a mattress on the floor.

Why did her cousin come to Geneva?
Uniquely in order to keep her company.

Did they go together yesterday morning to Laconnex?
Yes, they left at four thirty in the morning, just the two of them.

What were they intending to do in Laconnex?
They were going to settle things with the wet nurse and pay her salary for the months that had not yet been paid.

Did she enter the home of the wet nurse with her cousin?
Yes, her cousin never left her side between their arrival and their departure.

What room did they enter into first?
They were in the kitchen.

Whom did they speak to?
With the mother of the wet nurse[11] whom they found alone in the kitchen.

Was her child not in the room?
No, she was in an alcove, asleep in her crib.

When she arrived, did she ask for the wet nurse?
Yes.

Is it not true that the defendant sent for her and that it was the mother of the wet nurse who went to fetch her?
Yes, the mother of the wet nurse got her daughter out of the crib, put a white undershirt on her, and brought her to where she and Sieur de la Fléchère were sitting.

Was the child of the wet nurse also present?
Yes, he was with his grandmother.

---

[11] Louise Ducré, the mother-in-law of the wet nurse, is sometimes referred to simply as her "mother."

Did she not request that the mother of the wet nurse go fetch the wet nurse?
Yes, she thinks that it was the little boy who went.

Is it not true that she asked the mother of the wet nurse to go get her?
No, the mother of the wet nurse never left the room.

Did she not bring something for her child?
Yes, she brought her some candy and that morning, when leaving the city, she
    even turned back to buy some linens [for her], but she did not buy them
    because the shops were still closed.

Did she give candy to her child?
Yes, the deponent gave some to her while she was having her undershirt put on.
    She only gave her one piece of candy, which she held in her hand, and, at the
    same time, she gave one to the child of the wet nurse.

Did anyone else eat the candy?
The grandmother ate some.

During this time, did the children eat or drink anything else?
They did not eat or drink anything else while the grandmother held the little girl.

*Is it not true that at that moment she asked the mother of the wet nurse for a cup
    and that she gave her one?*
She never asked for a cup and the said woman never gave her one.

*Is it not true that she then asked for some wine and the woman told her that she
    would find some in the jug?*
No.

*Is it not true that the grandmother left the room to fetch her daughter and that
    when she did so she left the said little child with the deponent?*
Yes, it is true that the said grandmother gave her the child to finish dressing
    her, but she does not know whether the said woman left the room.

Who remained in the room at that time?
There was Sieur de la Fléchère, herself, her daughter, and the little boy whom
    she thinks went to get his mother.

*Is it not true that during this interval she gave something to drink to the two
    children?*
No, neither she nor Sieur de la Fléchère gave them anything to drink.

Did she not give more candy to the children as soon as the wet nurse arrived?
When the wet nurse arrived, she put the candy on the table. Both the said wet
    nurse and another man who arrived soon after ate some, as did the deponent
    and Sieur de la Fléchère.

Did they take candy of their own accord or did she tell them to have some?
She invited them to eat some.

How did her child seem when she first arrived?
She found her well, though it is true that the deponent noticed that her stomach was a little distended, which she attributed to her having worms.

In what state did she find the child of the wet nurse when she arrived in Laconnex?
She found him well and walking around.

Yet was it not these same two children who began to vomit?
The child of the wet nurse went outside and lay down on the ground and her daughter vomited a bit and then it seemed she stopped. But soon after it became clear that both children were vomiting and were having heart pains.

Did she notice what kind of vomiting it was? Were the children drooling, sticking out their tongues, and foaming at the mouth?
No.

Is it not true that the defendant then said that it was only the worms that were making them vomit and, in order to help them, they needed to be given some orviétan and have milk rubbed on their throats?
Yes, and so we gave them some *orviétan* and we rubbed milk on their throats.

Is it not true that once the said children were badly affected by the vomiting and they started to twitch that she said her own brother had died in Geneva of worms and that the physicians had not known what the illness was.
Yes, she did say that.

Is it not true that, seeing the children in such a state, the defendant said that she wished she had given an écu and wished she had not given that to the children?
She did say that.

Did she stay in Laconnex for long after the children began vomiting?
Since the children had fallen asleep, she left because her cousin pressured her to do so saying that his own father was very ill. The wet nurse led them out and accompanied them to the end of the orchard.

How is it that she abandoned her own child, who was in danger, and even more so the child of the wet nurse, who had the same sickness?
She felt she had to go because her cousin wanted to return to Geneva and she did not wish to remain in Laconnex all alone.

Why did she make a point of distributing candy to everyone in the house given that she had only brought a small amount for her daughter?

She is not in the habit of eating an apple in front of everyone without offering any and then having everyone watch her eat it herself.

Is it not true that the candy she gave the children was different from the sweets she and her cousin ate as well as those she offered to the wet nurse, her mother, and the other peasant?
No, and no one could say differently.

Is it not true that she gave the children a powder while the mother-in-law went to fetch her daughter-in-law the wet nurse?
No, but if anyone gave them a powder, it must have been the wet nurse.

Is it not true that about a year ago she sent some powder or tablets to her child and ordered the wet nurse to give them to her daughter?
No, but it is true that the husband of the wet nurse reported that a man on horseback, dressed in red wearing shoes with golden spurs, sent a servant with tablets or a powder for the child, but that the wet nurse did not want to give them to her child since the deponent had told her never to give anything to the child except by her order.

Is it not true that the husband of the wet nurse gave the tablets or powder to Sieur Gédéon Régis who then gave them to her?
Yes. Her brother, who is now dead, and the late Sieur Régis, who were suspicious that it was poison, bought a hen in order to test what effect the said powder or tablets would have. But the hen did not die and she lived another three months before they finally ate her.

Did Sieur Régis not ask her what effect the said powder or tablets had on the hen?
Yes, and she told him they had had no effect.

Did she not go several times to visit her daughter while she was being cared for by the wet nurse, notably one time when both she and her companion were dressed as servants?
Yes. It was her cousin Joanne de la Fléchère who accompanied her.

Is it not true that, after having given birth, she said that she prayed to God to take her child after she was baptized?
It is possible she said that since she also wanted to die.

What time did she and her cousin de la Fléchère arrive back in Geneva? Did he stay the night?
They arrived back around one o'clock, ate a salad together in her room, and then her cousin left to return to Nyon about two o'clock.

Is it not true that she and her cousin, seeing how sick the children were, left Laconnex before they had finished eating?

No, she did not leave until the children were sleeping.

Before she left Geneva, did she tell Mademoiselle Fabri where she was going?
No.

Did she not tell her the night before when she bought the candy from her that it was to bring to her child?
No, she had never told her that she had a child in Laconnex.

When she returned to Geneva, did she tell Damoiselle Fabri that she was coming back from Laconnex?
No.

Is it not true that Damoiselle Fabri told her to leave the city because it was dangerous for her to remain and that she asked the defendant whether she had been to Laconnex?
Yes, but the deponent replied that she was shocked to hear what people were saying about her, she did not know what she would do if she left, she was not guilty of anything, and she did not want to leave town.

Is it not true that, having been advised to flee by Damoiselle Fabri, she immediately started to do so and left heading in the direction of the Boulevard?
She went searching for a woman who could accompany her to Laconnex to see what had happened, having already asked the said Damoiselle Fabri to give her her servant.

Did she come across the husband of the wet nurse in town?
Yes, when returning to the home of Damoiselle Fabri. He told her that she needed to come talk to Monsieur the *Auditeur* to answer questions about the death of the children that she had caused by giving them something to eat.

Is it not true that she said to the husband of the wet nurse and to his uncle, who was accompanying him, that they should not speak of what had happened and that they should come up to her room?
She did ask them to come up to her room and not to make such a loud ruckus because people would think the wrong thing, but denies the implication of the interrogator.

Summoned to declare whether it is not true that the children died of poison and that it was discovered that she gave them the poison by means of a drink or powder while she and Sieur de la Fléchère were alone in the kitchen with them.
She never gave any poison to the children, if they were poisoned at all, and God should take her had she even thought of doing so.

Is it not true that she caused the death of her child in order to relieve herself of the
responsibility of caring for her and in order to hide that she had had a child?
She never entertained such an idea and the wet nurse knows the efforts she
made to care for her child and the lengths she went to support her and
ensure that she never lacked anything.

Summoned to reveal who the real father of the child was.
She does not think it is necessary to tell them.

Summoned once again to declare whether she recognizes having committed a
major crime by committing fornication, by hiding her pregnancy, by giving
birth secretly, by hiding the existence of her child, and by causing the death of
her child and of another child by means of poison she gave to them.
She admits having committed a grave sin with regards to the fornication, for
which she asked and continues to ask God for pardon, but she is innocent of
the poisoning.

That she then declare who she thinks might have given the children poison and on
whom she casts suspicion since there is no one else who could have done this
crime given that the children were overcome with convulsions of vomiting and
died so soon after she left Laconnex.
She does not wish to cast aspersions on anyone, but if the children do have
poison in their stomachs, she was not the person who gave it to them, and, if
ever she had such sinister thoughts, God should take her and she would have
killed the child while she was still in her stomach.

Summoned to tell the truth.
Declared having done so.
Jane Thomaset [*sic*]

The answers given here by Thomasset were recorded in the prison in the
presence of Monsieur Lieutenant of Justice, and *auditeurs* Bagueret, Gautier,
and Du Puy.

Galiffe, clerk

—————————————— **FOLIO 12** ——————————————

[May 8, 1686. Deliberations of the Small Council. The Small Council decided
to write to Noble Nicolas Steiguer, bailiff of Nyon, the chief judicial and mili-
tary officer in the district of the Vaud where Daniel de la Fléchère lived. We
do not have the letter the council sent, but it is likely that it asked the bailiff to
send de la Fléchère to Geneva for questioning.]

Saturday, May 8, 1686.[12] The entire council present. Lieutenant of justice present.

Jeanne Thomasset of Orbe, prisoner suspected of having poisoned her own bastard child, who was being cared for in Laconnex, as well as the son of the wet nurse. She was accompanied to Laconnex by Daniel de la Fléchère of Nyon. The council examined her testimony given in the council chamber and in prison given before the lieutenant, the reports of the *auditeurs*, the report of the physicians and surgeons who examined the corpses, the witness testimony collected by the *châtelain* of St. Victor, as well as the declarations made by Abraham Clerc and Pierre Quiby, both of Laconnex, regarding the criminal complaint made by the said Clerc, father of the poisoned boy. It was decided that the council go today to the prison to pursue the investigation and, at the same time, write to the Lord Bailiff of Nyon to inform him with regards to Daniel de la Fléchère, over whom he has jurisdiction. The letter [to the bailiff of Nyon] was read to the council and approved.

──────────────── **FOLIO 13** ────────────────

[May 7–8, 1686. Report of the Auditeur Bagueret describing his visit to the home of Damoiselle Fabri and his search of Jeanne Catherine's bedchamber.]

I, the undersigned *auditeur*, certify that, by the order of Monsieur Lieutenant of Justice, I directly transported myself to the Place Bourg-de-Four, specifically to the home of the widow of the late Noble Urbain Fabri, where Thomasset rented a room, to receive the deposition of the said Damoiselle widow Fabri, which I submitted to the Lord Lieutenant that day. Subsequently and by the same order, I asked the said Damoiselle Fabri to hand over whatever remained of the candy that she had sold to the said Thomasset. I then asked her if the bedchamber of the said Thomasset was unlocked. She said that it was not, but that she had a key in her possession. I ordered her to accompany me to the chamber, which she did, and, having opened the door and opened a trunk that was within, I examined everything in the chamber, including the trunk, boxes, cordials, linens, and toiletries to see if I could find the remainder of the candy or anything else that could be poison. In the course of this search, I found nothing but a red powder wrapped in paper and, in another paper, a yellow substance that I did not recognize. Within the trunk, I also found several letters addressed to the

────────────
[12]   AEG RC 186, f. 137.

said Thomasset by various different people, including some copies written in a woman's hand and other letters, all of which I handed over to the lieutenant who has read them. Having returned the objects as they had been before, I locked the trunk and will keep both the key to the trunk and the key to the bedchamber until otherwise instructed. Undertaken in Geneva the 7th May, 1686.

Bagueret, auditeur

May 8, 1686. Having received an order from Monsieur the Lieutenant to take the two substances wrapped in paper mentioned above and have them examined by a licensed apothecary, I removed them from the trunk in Thomasset's room and took them to licensed apothecary Pierre Roy. I showed them to him and he examined them, reporting to me that the red powder is tobacco leaves and the yellow substance is slightly rancid rabbit grease, this being what he declared to me on the said day.

Bagueret, auditeur

FOLIO 14

[March 11, 1685. Letter written by Jeanne Catherine Thomasset to an unknown recipient over a year before the trial. The letter was presumably never sent since it was found among her possessions when Auditeur Bagueret confiscated personal effects from her room in the widow Fabri's home on May 8. Jeanne Catherine makes reference to a Mademoiselle de la Fléchère in the letter, likely her cousin Joanne de la Fléchère who accompanied her once to Laconnex.]

I am sorry to write you so often about the same matter, but, seeing as you have never answered me, I can only conclude that you have not received my letters. I beseech you to respond to this one and to tell me whether what this great man owes me has been obtained so that I can keep my creditors at bay, for I find myself in a difficult situation. You are too reasonable to allow these debts to hound me; it is easy to see that I need all manner of things, since you know thirty *écus* is not enough to sustain two people for a year. My dear Sieur, I beseech you to treat me charitably and to provide me with all that was rightly promised to me; I will send the letter to you. If you cannot extend this goodwill and charity toward me, I will be forced to seek help from someone else and show them my correspondence such that they will give me what is necessary for my subsistence since, in good conscience, nothing at all has as

yet been provided to me by my family. Judge for yourself what state I am reduced to. I beg you, in the name of God, for everything, even though it is only
what I had been promised. I pray to God that He bless you and your family.

March 11, 1685.

[on the reverse side of the page]

Mademoiselle de la Fléchère will deliver this letter directly to you. She must
return to Geneva next Friday. You can entrust your response to her in whatever manner you see fit. Your very humble servant J.C.T.

───────────────────────── **FOLIO 15** ─────────────────────────

*[April 13, 1685. Letter addressed to Jeanne Catherine written by her brother
Samuel the previous year, presumably confiscated by Auditeur Bagueret. In it,
Samuel makes repeated reference to Romainmôtier, the district in the Vaud
region in which Agiez and Orbe were located. The bailiff there had been enlisted
by the Thomasset family to advocate on behalf of Jeanne Catherine with the
authorities in Bern. Samuel Thomasset later lived with Jeanne Catherine in
Geneva and died there in March 1686, just two months before the trial.]*

Agiez, April 13, 1685.

To Mademoiselle Jeanne Catherine Thomasset
Pâquis, Geneva

We were very surprised, my dear sister, when we arrived from Bules not to find
you at the house, but it seems that our local minister was the cause [of your
departure] since he warned Monsieur the Bailiff as soon as he learned that you
had arrived. My sister, S. found this out from a man he sent to report back to
us. Our father must speak to Monsieur the Bailiff about the letter of support
he wrote [on your behalf]. He [the bailiff] responded that he would warn the
High Consistory[13] in Bern and that he [our father] might be called to act as
a witness. Our father said he would go to Bern if summoned and he would
have arguments to bring forward. He repeated what you had said in front of
Monsieur de Crose [a cousin], that you would rather be drawn and quartered
than be pressured into saying anything more than you have already said. One

─────────────────

[13] A church court that judged sex crimes such as fornication.

should never do oneself wrong in order to please one's enemies and we should collect more information where the events took place. I strongly encourage you to act as soon as possible on what you planned when you wrote to cousin Rose; this would please you know who. It is by no means certain, however, that this business will go that far. Our mother hopes that what she has proposed will come to pass because she believes that the situation will stay as is and that we will hear no more of it. Monsieur the Bailiff left for Bern on Sunday for Easter and to do business there for three weeks. I do not know if he will do what he told my father he would do, but he [our father] does not fear the men who are talking about it, saying that we can do nothing about the letter. I believe we will return at the beginning of the month of May. Be happy and do not worry. You must trust all to the Providence of God and believe that he will grant us grace to vanquish our enemies. Adieu, my dear sister, I am yours truly, your brother and your servant, and will be for the rest of my life, S. Thomasset.

Please send good wishes to our Régis cousins. Write us again soon.

My mother offers greetings to the Régis cousins and hopes they will continue their kindness to us.

Our mother, our sister, our brother and I, as well as Monsieur Margel and our sister all say hello.

You have sent your red underskirt to Aunt Eschaquet instead of your riding skirt. Try to get it to her as soon as possible.

[Along the margin:] we will write you soon as needed.

FOLIO 16

[May 8, 1686. Third interrogation of Jeanne Catherine Thomasset.]

Testimony of Jeanne, about twenty-six years old, daughter of Sieur Jean François Thomasset of Orbe, in the Vaud.

Did she give birth to a child left in Laconnex to be nursed?
Yes, about two years ago.

What is the name of the person with whom she left her child?
She does not know the name of the husband but the wife is named Jeanne Marie.

Has she gone to visit her child often?
Three or four times, but the last time she went, last Thursday, she was accompanied by her cousin Daniel de la Fléchère of Nyon.

Who did she encounter in Laconnex in the house where her child was staying?
Only the mother of the wet nurse.

Where was her child?
In the crib.

Was there not another child?
There were two other children of the wet nurse, one of them in the room and
the other outside.

Did she get her child out of the crib?
The mother of the wet nurse did so.

<u>*Did she then take the child in her arms?*</u>
The mother of the wet nurse got her up and put an undershirt on her, but since
the child did not want to be dressed, the deponent gave her a candy she had
brought with her.

<u>*Once the child was out of the crib, did she not send for the wet nurse?*</u>
She only asked the mother of the wet nurse where the wet nurse was, and, at
that, the child who was outside went to fetch her from the garden.

<u>*Did she not order the mother of the wet nurse to go get her?*</u>
She is not sure whether the mother of the wet nurse went to get her and
whether it was by her order. She cannot recall precisely.

<u>*Once her child was out of the crib, did she not ask the mother of the wet nurse for
a cup and some wine?*</u>
No, and no one brought her any wine or a cup, since one does not need one
without the other.

<u>*Did the mother of the wet nurse not tell her that there was wine in the jug?*</u>
No.

<u>*Did she not remain alone in the room with her cousin and the two children when
the mother of the wet nurse went to fetch the wet nurse?*</u>
She did not pay any attention because her child was sitting on her lap.

<u>*Did the wet nurse take long to arrive?*</u>
Her child was not yet dressed when the wet nurse arrived.

<u>*Did she not give something to the children before the wet nurse arrived?*</u>
No, and she gave nothing to the children in the presence of anyone in the
household, except for the candy.

<u>*Soon after the wet nurse arrived, did the children not begin to froth at the mouth
and vomit?*</u>

The children were sitting at the table when her daughter began to vomit and the wet nurse said that it was likely the worms were agitated by the sweetness of the candy, and, since the deponent had also concluded as much, she then asked the wet nurse if she did not have something to ease the child's pain and she gave her some *orviétan* in a spoon with some wine.

Did the other child not react similarly?
The said child went outside to lie on the ground and when his mother went to get him, she also gave him some *orviétan* in a spoon.

Did she not give anything else to the children other than the candy?
No and the wet nurse remarked on this.

Given that the children had not had anything else to eat, is it not likely that the candy caused this rapid reaction?
She was very surprised.

Did her cousin always remain close by?
Yes.

How is it that the deponent left her child while she was so ill?
When she left, her child was sleeping, which led her to think that the illness would not continue, and also her cousin was pressuring her to leave.

Who was in the house when she left Laconnex?
The wet nurse, the mother of the wet nurse, and another man, brother of the wet nurse.

Was she not requested and pressured to remain until it was determined what was causing the distress of the children?
No, but she did say that if she had someone to accompany her back to Geneva that she would stay, but everyone was also hoping that the illness was not serious.

Were the children vomiting and experiencing convulsions while the adults were eating?
No, the wet nurse had set aside an egg for her daughter, which she gave to her.

Did the deponent and her cousin finish their meal? Did they not get up from the table before they were done?
No, they had entirely finished their meal, after which everyone left the table and the brother of the wet nurse went out into the courtyard.

When they returned to Geneva, did her cousin leave immediately?
No, he did some errands in town and then returned shortly afterwards to her bedchamber where he had a salad and then left.

How long did they stay at the home of the wet nurse in Laconnex?
They left Geneva about half past four in the morning and returned about one in
the afternoon.

Did the sickness of the children begin long before lunch?
It started soon after her daughter was dressed.

Did the sickness of the other child start at the same time as that of her daughter?
Since he went outside to lie on the ground, his symptoms started shortly after.

*Soon after her return to Geneva, did a peasant not come to tell her that the
children had been poisoned?*
Yes, she was very surprised and was obliged to tell him that if he had something
to say to her that they should go upstairs together.

Did she go out soon after her cousin left?
She went to the rooms of the Damoiselles Mollat who live in the same house.

Where did she go with her umbrella?
Since she was going to the pastry shop after visiting Damoiselle Rey, the latter
lent the deponent an umbrella to protect her from the rain.

What route did she take to return home?
Through the courtyard of St. Pierre Cathedral, then along the alley of [...],
which ends at the Place Bourg-de-Four.

Summoned to tell the truth about the deaths of the children.
She is completely innocent.

*Did Mademoiselle Fabri not speak to her shortly before the arrival of the peasant
to warn her to leave town?*
Yes, Damoiselle Fabri asked her whether she had been to Laconnex, and, when
she answered, she asked her what she had been doing there. Damoiselle Fabri
told the deponent that bad rumors were circulating and it would be best for
her to leave the city. The deponent responded that if Damoiselle Fabri lent
her a servant, she would go to Laconnex. Damoiselle Fabri told her that her
servant was not home, which obliged the deponent to go to the Boulevard
Saint-Antoine to find her. When she was not able to do so, she retraced her
steps and ran into the peasant.

Did she stay at the home of her cousin de la Fléchère in Nyon?
No, at the home of her Aunt Damond.

Why did her cousin accompany her to Geneva?
To keep her company.

Was the father of her cousin sick?
He had a headache.

While in Laconnex was her cousin ever alone with the children?
No, they were always together.

What time did they arrive on Wednesday from Nyon?
It was already late.

When they left Nyon, had they already decided to visit Laconnex?
No, they only decided that evening while having supper.

Was the candy that she gave the children made with ordinary sugar?
Yes.

Was it shortly after giving the children the candy that they fell ill?
It was shortly after her daughter was dressed.

Seeing her child sick, did she not say that she thought that she had worms?
Yes.

<u>*Did she not say that the candy she gave the children was good for treating worms?*</u>
<u>No.</u>

Did she not know that the children were sick from poison?
She has heard it said, and she finds this very surprising.

<u>*Did she not say that she wished she had given them an écu and not given them the candy?*</u>
<u>Yes, because she thought that the sugar had produced this effect, the sweetness having caused the worms to rise to the back of their throats.</u>

Had she not gone to a shop to buy some things?
No, except to the shop of Damoiselle Fabri where she bought the candy.

Is her cousin married?
Yes.

<u>*When she went in the direction of Saint-Antoine, did she not find the passageway blocked?*</u>
<u>No.</u>

Is it true that a child of the wet nurse was outside of the house?
Yes, and it was a boy.

Did she not tell the wet nurse that she had given something to the children that was good for worms?
No.

Did she not say that she wished that her daughter was dead?
She does not believe she ever said that.

Why did she deny to Mademoiselle Fabri that she had gone to Laconnex?
So that she would not know that the deponent had a child.

<u>*One year ago, did she not send a powder to the wet nurse to give to her daughter?*</u>
<u>No.</u>

<u>*Did the wet nurse not bring the powder back to her?*</u>
<u>Yes, she said that a man had sent it and asked whether her daughter had any linens.</u>

With whom did she have the said daughter?
[blank space]

Where did her cousin sleep Wednesday night before they went to Laconnex?
In the bedchamber of the deponent.

Who is the father of her child? Summoned to tell the truth.
She will answer if you name him.

Was it her cousin Roch?
It is all too true.

Does her cousin de la Fléchère know who the father is?
She thinks he does.

Did she not write to her father and mother, or to other relatives saying, if they did not help her, that she would cause them distress?
She does not believe that she ever wrote anything of the kind.

FOLIO 17

[May 10, 1686. Deliberations of the Small Council regarding its correspondence with the bailiff of Nyon about Jeanne Catherine's cousin Daniel de la Fléchère.]

Monday, May 10, 1686.[14]

Monsieur Steiguer, bailiff of Nyon. Have seen his letter in response [to ours] from the 9th of this month, in which he thanked the council for the

---

[14] AEG RC 186, f. 138.

information concerning Daniel de la Fléchère and said that he would pass
it along to the council at Bern.

FOLIO 18

[May 10, 1686. Fourth interrogation of Jeanne Catherine Thomasset.]

*Did she not go to Laconnex with Sieur de la Fléchère last Thursday to see her
child?*
Yes.

What time did they arrive?
She does not know.

Who was in the house when she arrived?
The mother of the wet nurse and her child, who was in a crib, and another
child, who was also in a crib.

Did she get her daughter up?
Yes, the mother of the wet nurse got her up, put an undershirt on her, and
started to lace her and then gave the child to the deponent to finish up.

Did someone get the other child up?
The wet nurse got him up when she returned.

Was there not another child, a boy four or five years old?
He was not in the room at first, but he entered soon afterwards.

*What did the mother of the wet nurse do after she gave her the child? Did she stay
in the room or did she leave?*
She cannot recall whether she stayed in the room or whether she left with her
daughter's dirty undershirt.

Did she not ask for the wet nurse?
Yes, and the mother told her that she was in the garden and even asked the
deponent whether she had seen her when she came through the orchard.

Who went to get the wet nurse?
She does not know whether it was the mother of the wet nurse or the child.

*How is it possible that she was in the room and that she did not notice whether the
mother had left?*
She was by the fire very much preoccupied with lacing up her daughter and so
she did not turn around to look.

Did she not ask the mother of the wet nurse for a cup and some wine?
No.

Did the said woman not give her a cup and tell her that there was wine in the jug?
No, how would she be able to give her a cup and the wine while she was busy
holding her child and trying to dress her?

Did she not ask where the wet nurse was?
Yes, but she did not tell her to go and get her.

Did it take long for the wet nurse to arrive?
Seven or eight minutes, while she finished lacing up and dressing the child.

What did she give to the children?
She gave them nothing, except a candy to her child while they were putting on
her undershirt, and some candy to the other boy.

When the wet nurse arrived, did the children not start to vomit?
Her daughter was already feeling sick when she was being dressed and her
stomach was distended.

Were the children not vomiting and frothing at the mouth?
They were certainly vomiting, but they were not frothing at the mouth.

What did she say to the wet nurse when she saw the children in such a state?
They both said that it must be the worms that were rising to their throats and the
wet nurse said that on another occasion she had put herbs on their stomachs.

Did they not give them [the children] something to drink and to eat?
Yes, and she ate a spoonful of milk and an egg.

Seeing her child in such a bad way, why did she leave so soon?
When they left, the children were sleeping quietly and they did not think that
the sickness was very serious and also her cousin was in a rush to return.

Did they leave the house alone?
The wet nurse accompanied them to the end of the orchard.

What time did she arrive back in town?
At one in the afternoon and she went directly back to her bedchamber.

Where did her cousin go?
He joined her shortly afterwards and they ate together in her chamber.

Did Mademoiselle Fabri not ask her whether she had been to Laconnex that day?
Yes, and she replied that it was none of her business.

Did the said Damoiselle not tell her that bad rumors were circulating?
Yes, and she advised her to leave.

Where did she go after that?

She asked Damoiselle Fabri to lend her a servant in order to go to Laconnex to find out what had happened. But the servant was not at home, so she went to look for another woman on the ramparts. When she could not find her, she returned home.

When returning home, did she not encounter a peasant, husband to the wet nurse, who grabbed her by the arm saying that she had caused the death of the two children?

Yes, and she told him that he should keep quiet and come up to her bedchamber.

While on the ramparts, did she not take the path to the Rive gate in order to leave the city?

Yes, with the intention of finding the servant that she was looking for whom she had been told was on that side of town.

Sometime ago, did she not send some tablets and some powder to give to her child?

No.

Was the said powder not returned to Monsieur Régis who gave it to her?

Yes, the wet nurse returned it to the deponent in order to find out whether it was true that she had sent it.

When she abandoned her child so quickly, was it not because people were starting to say that she had been poisoned?

She swears to God that it was not.

Did she not say that she wished she had given them an écu and wished that she had not given the children what she gave them?

No.[15]

Did the child of the wet nurse not say that he had not eaten anything except that which the said Damoiselle had given him?

She did not hear him say that.

Did she not say that if they had all not eaten some candy, one might say that it was the candy that had poisoned the said children?

No.

---

[15] In the margins of the original manuscript, it is noted that this reply contradicts a previous statement made by Jeanne Catherine.

Who was the woman she was looking for?
A woman named Pernette.

───────────────────── **FOLIO 19** ─────────────────────

[May 10, 1686. Testimony of Louise Ducré, mother-in-law of the wet nurse, taken in Geneva.]

Testimony of Louise Ducré, widow of Étienne Clerc of Laconnex, does not know her age.

Where does she live?
In Laconnex at the home of her son Abraham Clerc with his wife Jeanne Marie Favre.

Does her daughter-in-law not nurse a child?
Yes, she nursed a girl, who was the daughter of a woman who claimed to be from the Vaud region, but who was otherwise unknown to her.

Did the mother of the girl come often to visit her?
Two or three times.

When was the last time she came to visit?
One day last week, she does not remember which day, but it was in the morning.

Did she arrive alone?
She arrived with a young man whom she said was her cousin.

Was the deponent the only person in the house when they arrived?
Yes. The child of her daughter-in-law and the child of the Damoiselle were still in bed.

Where were her son and her daughter-in-law?
Her son was out working and her daughter was at the fountain washing the children's clothes.

What did the said Damoiselle say when she arrived?
A moment after the said Damoiselle arrived, her daughter woke up and the deponent went to get her out of the crib, then put a white undershirt on her and then her dress, at which point the said Damoiselle asked the deponent to give her the child to finish dressing her while the deponent went to call the wet nurse.

Did the said Damoiselle ask for nothing else after having told her to get the wet nurse?
She asked for a cup and for some wine without saying what she would do with them.

Did she give her the cup and the wine?
Yes, she gave her a cup made of wood and a jug containing red wine from the day before and then went to get her daughter the wet nurse.

Did she not say why she wanted the wine?
No and she also did not see what the Damoiselle did with it.

Between her leaving and her return, was anyone but the said Damoiselle and her cousin with the children?
No.

Was the child of the wet nurse also out of bed when she left to fetch the wet nurse?
Yes, she got him up after the other one.

Is it far from the house to the fountain?
She could not say precisely but it might be the same as the distance between the tower of the Arve and the station of the captain of the guard.

When she gave the cup and the jug to the said Damoiselle, was the cousin present and did he see her doing so?
Yes.

Did her daughter-in-law return to the house right away when she called her?
Yes, they returned together.

When they returned, what state were the children in?
They found them starting to vomit, the girl while sitting on her mother's lap, and her daughter's child on the threshold.

What did the said Damoiselle say when she saw the children in such a state?
She said may it please God that we did not give that to them; if the other girl had been here, she might have reacted the same.

Did she say what she had given the children?
No, though she did say that it was a remedy to cure worms and added that it would do no good, that if they came to the city, she would give them a powder to cure the worms.

Did she see the said Thomasset give anything else to the children?
Before she asked for the cup and the wine, the deponent did see her give each of the children a sweet. And the deponent also ate one of them.

Did the brother of her daughter-in-law named Favre arrive long after the children started to vomit?
He arrived soon after they started vomiting.

Did the said Damoiselle and her cousin eat anything?
We provided them with some fried eggs, but they only drank some milk because, once they saw the children vomiting, they got up from the table and left, the young man saying that his father was sick so that he had to leave right away. She did not see or hear the said Thomasset making any effort to stay near her sick daughter.

Was the brother of her daughter-in-law not at the table with them?
No, he only had a drink while standing.

Did he leave with the said Damoiselle and her cousin?
No, he stayed sometime longer, she thinks perhaps until the children died.

Did he not say he would be in the courtyard?
She does not remember.

<u>*Did the children linger long after they became ill?*</u>
<u>Half an hour.</u>

Did the child of her daughter-in-law know how to talk?
Yes.

<u>*Did he not talk about feeling ill?*</u>
<u>Yes, when he was asked how he was feeling and what he had eaten, he replied that he had only eaten what the said Damoiselle had given him to eat and to drink in the cup.</u>

<u>*Who was present when the child said this?*</u>
<u>The wet nurse, who posed the question, and the said Favre, her brother.</u>

Did the deponent or the others who were helping not say anything to the said Damoiselle when they saw the children in such a state?
They were all upset and then the said Damoiselle told them to give the children some *orviétan* and to go get something from the garden to give them as well.

Was that done?
She does not remember if they gave the children some *orviétan*, but the deponent went to fetch some garlic from the garden to rub on their throats.

<u>*Was the said Damoiselle present when the garlic was rubbed on the children?*</u>
<u>Yes, but seeing the children in such a desperate state, she left right away.</u>

Did any member of the household accompany the said Damoiselle and her cousin when they left the house?
No, they were busy taking care of the children.

When they left in this way, did no one think to accuse them and did anyone say anything to them?
No, because we could not imagine that they would do any harm.

Were the children sleeping when they left?
No, they were still in the kitchen and they did not stop vomiting.

Was there any rat poison in the house?
No, they never kept any.

Did anyone else drink from the said cup?
No, everyone else drank from a glass.

What happened to the wooden cup?
She does not know.
Testimony read aloud, witness confirmed testimony.

FOLIO 20

[May 10, 1686. Testimony of Jeanne Marie Favre of Laconnex, mother of the dead boy, given in the city council chambers in Geneva.]

Testimony of Jeanne Marie Favre, wife of Abraham Clerc, about twenty-six years old.

Was she not nursing a child for a Damoiselle?
Yes, she took care of her for two years and one month.

Does she know the name of the said Damoiselle?
No.

Did the said Damoiselle often come to visit her child?
Three times, the last time was last week. She is not certain of the exact day, though since then someone told her that it was Thursday, and she arrived with a middle-aged man, about thirty to forty years of age.

What time did they arrive?
About seven in the morning.

Was she at the house when they arrived?

No, she was at the fountain, which is about as far from the house as from here to the courtyard of the St. Pierre Cathedral. Her mother found her there after having looked for her in a house between their home and the fountain where the said Damoiselle gave birth to the child.

When she left for the fountain, who was in the house?
Her mother-in-law and the children, but when she returned she found the said Damoiselle, the Monsieur, and the children, who were out of bed, the child of the said Damoiselle sitting in her lap and her own child close by.

In what condition did she find the children?
She found them pale and, a moment later, they started to vomit, first one, then the other, at which point the said Damoiselle said one should not be surprised, that it was probably worms, and that she or her husband should come to Geneva to fetch a powder for worms to give to them in red wine.

Did she at any point notice the said Damoiselle giving anything to the children?
No, except for the candy. The Damoiselle said that the child of the deponent ate more of them than did her daughter. As the sickness of the children continued, the man who accompanied the said Damoiselle started to put pressure on her to leave, saying that he had to return that same day to visit his father who was sick and that if the Damoiselle wanted to stay she should give him the keys to her bedchamber. Putting them on the table, the said Damoiselle said she wanted very much to stay and see what was wrong with the children. But she did decide to leave with the said Monsieur and she said she wanted to give them an *écu* and wished she had not given something to the children and that the sugar made the worms rise up against their hearts and that her brother had died of this same sickness without the physicians being able to diagnose it.

Was her child not able to speak?
When he was questioned by his father, he said that he had a stomachache and that he had eaten nothing but that which the said Damoiselle had given him, without specifying what that was.

Did she not hear anyone say that the Damoiselle had given the children something to drink?
No.

Did they have wine in the house?
Yes.

Was there some wine left in the jug?
She does not know.

Does she know if the said Damoiselle asked for wine and a cup when she arrived?

She heard her mother-in-law saying that the Damoiselle had done so.

Did she notice whether the said Damoiselle was taking care of her child?

The deponent was paying attention and can verify that the Damoiselle was taking good care of her daughter.

Did she offer anything to eat to the visitors?

She gave them some eggs and some milk and went to fetch some white wine from the local tavern, but they had no patience for eating, except the milk and to take a drink, without ever eating the eggs. Her brother was standing near the table and she thinks he also had a drink with them.

When the Damoiselle and her companion left, did the deponent not accompany them?

She accompanied them to the end of the orchard. As they were leaving, the deponent said she would come to town the next day to get a powder for curing worms, but the man who was with her said that there was no point in coming before next Wednesday when the moon would be waning.

Once they left, did she give the children anything to drink or eat?

She only gave them *orviétan* with a bit of wine, which they had some trouble keeping down.

When the said Damoiselle left, were the children sleeping?

Yes, it seemed that they were sleeping, but they were simply exhausted and soon started vomiting again.

Before going to the fountain, had she given them anything to eat?

No.

Had anyone died in her home before this?

No.

Did the said Damoiselle pay her the wages she was owed and did she talk about settling the account?

She gave her an *écu* and told her to come to Geneva Wednesday to the widow Jeanne's home where she would pay her the rest and would give her an advance for an entire year.

Did the deponent not say to the said Damoiselle that she wanted to keep [taking care of] the child?

The Damoiselle said that she wanted to remove her child [from the wet nurse's care] and the deponent replied that the Damoiselle should be careful to place her daughter well. The deponent wanted to continue to care for the child, but the said Damoiselle did not seem to want her to.

Is it not true that some time ago the said Damoiselle sent her some tablets and a powder?
About a year ago, a girl, whom she did not recognize, came to the house bringing tablets and a powder to give to the child, but the deponent did not want to do so, and so she gave the powder and tablets to Sieur Régis.

Testimony read aloud and witness confirmed it.

FOLIO 21

[May 10, 1686. Testimony of Pierre Favre, maternal uncle of the deceased boy, given at the city council chambers in Geneva. Favre arrived at the Clerc home in Laconnex the morning the children fell ill. He was the only male villager present when the children fell ill.]

Testimony of Pierre, son of Louis Favre of Avully, aged about thirty-five years.

Was he not at his brother-in-law's house in Laconnex last Thursday?
Yes.

Whom did he meet at the house?
He met a Monsieur and a Damoiselle whose child his sister used to nurse.

What were they doing when he arrived?
They were at the table and he stopped a moment with them. They had some soft-boiled eggs and fried eggs and he saw them eating and drinking.

Did they finish eating and drinking?
He left before they did.

Did he see the state the children were in?
At the entrance, he found his sister's little boy vomiting. Once he entered, he saw that the other little girl was also sick.

What were the Monsieur and the Damoiselle saying?
They were both astonished and the Damoiselle said that if they all had not eaten the candy she would have said there was something in it, but it was only worms and that they needed to go fetch something in the garden to give to them and rub onto them. Milk was brought and the children were rubbed

with it and given some *orviétan*, and the said Damoiselle gave it to the children with the wet nurse.

Did he hear anyone say that the little boy's sickness came on after someone gave [a remedy] to him?
He did not hear anyone say that.

Once her daughter fell ill, did he hear the said Damoiselle say that she did not want to leave and that she wanted to see how the illness developed?
Her cousin was insisting that he had to return and she told him that she wanted to wait in order to find out what would happen to the children.

Did he hear anyone say that the said Damoiselle gave something else to the children?
When the officials came to question his sister and mother-in-law, he heard the grandmother say that the said Damoiselle had asked her for a cup with some wine, and that she had given it to her.

FOLIO 22

[May 10, 1686. Confrontation between Jeanne Catherine Thomasset and Louise Ducré, widow of Étienne Clerc, grandmother of the dead boy. A confrontation was a judicial procedure in which the suspect was asked questions in the presence of one of the key witnesses for the prosecution in order to test the ability of the suspect to maintain their innocence.]

Asked the said Thomasset if it were not true that as soon as her daughter was fetched from the crib, she sent the mother of the wet nurse to fetch her at the fountain?
She simply asked where the wet nurse was to which the said Ducré answered that she was in the garden and asked if the deponent had not seen her while passing through the orchard.
The said Ducré reaffirmed her [own] testimony.

Asked the said Thomasset if it were not true that before the said Ducré went to fetch the wet nurse, she asked her for a cup and some wine and that the said Ducré gave her the cup and a jug in which there was wine?
No. She asked neither for some wine nor for a cup. The said Ducré handed her nothing.

The said Ducré reaffirmed her [own] testimony.
Asked the said Ducré if the said Thomasset was present when the child of the wet nurse was asked what was wrong and what he had eaten to which he replied that he had only eaten what the said Thomasset had given him.

No. She had already left.

Asked the said Ducré if the said Thomasset gave the children anything to drink in her presence.

No. Before going to fetch the wet nurse, the said Thomasset asked her for a cup and some wine whereupon she went to take a cup and a jug that was on the table by the stove and gave the cup into her hand and placed the jug on the hearth near the fire and then went to fetch the wet nurse.

The said Thomasset emphatically denied having asked for either the cup or the wine and denied that anything was brought to her.

Again, asked the said Ducré when exactly the said Thomasset asked her for the cup and the wine, and whether it was before going to fetch the wet nurse and before the children fell ill.

It was before.

Again the said Thomasset denied having ever asked for a cup or wine until it was necessary to administer the *orviétan* to the children and by that time the wet nurse had arrived.

The said Ducré continued to maintain that the said Thomasset had indeed asked for the wine and the cup before she went to the fountain, having also asked for wine a second time when the children were vomiting in order to give them *orviétan*.

--------------------------------- **FOLIO 23** ---------------------------------

[May 11, 1686. Deliberations of the Small Council.]

Tuesday, May 11, 1686.[16] The entire council present. Lieutenant of justice present.

Jeanne Thomasset, prisoner accused of poisoning. Having heard her previous testimony, the council decided that she will be questioned today in the torture chamber.

--------------------------------- **FOLIO 24** ---------------------------------

[May 11, 1686. Fifth interrogation of Jeanne Catherine Thomasset, first interrogation in the torture chamber.]

---

[16] AEG RC 186, f. 140.

Did she not go to Laconnex last Thursday to visit her daughter who was being nursed there?
Yes. With her cousin, Daniel de la Fléchère.

Who did they see when they entered the house?
Only the grandmother.

Where was her child?
In the crib.

When the mother of the wet nurse got the children up, did the deponent not request that the child be handed over to her to finish dressing her?
Yes.

Why did she take the child onto her lap in order to finish dressing her?
The grandmother gave her the child after changing her undershirt.

While she had the child on her lap, was she not alone with her cousin?
She did not notice whether the mother of the wet nurse had left.

Did she not ask the mother of the wet nurse to go fetch her daughter?
No. She only asked her where the wet nurse was.

Before the mother of the wet nurse left the room, did she not ask her for a cup?
No. She did not ask her for anything at all and, as a result, the mother of the wet nurse never handed anything to her.

Did she not also ask for some wine?
No.

Was the mother of the wet nurse away for long?
She does not know if the mother of the wet nurse left.

While she had her daughter on her lap, did the child of the wet nurse not approach her?
No, he had already left the house and she only saw him when he returned later.

While her daughter was sitting on her lap, did she not give some poison or some other substance that caused her death?
No. She only gave her some candy that she had bought from Madame Fabri.

Did she not also give some poison to the child of the wet nurse?
No, God protect her.

Did the wet nurse arrive soon after the deponent's entrance into the house?
She does not remember very well.

Did the children not start to vomit soon after the wet nurse arrived?
Yes.

What did the deponent do after she finished dressing her daughter?
She and her cousin went over to the hearth to eat since they had prepared some
   fried eggs, some soft-boiled eggs, and some milk.

When the children started to vomit, what did she say to the wet nurse?
The deponent told her that it was the worms.

Did she give them something for the worms?
She had only given them some candy.

Did they not give a remedy to the children?
The deponent asked if they had any *thériaque* at which point the wet nurse went
   to get some *orviétan*.

Given that her daughter was also sick, why did she leave Laconnex?
When she left, her child was sleeping peacefully.

<u>*Why did she not finish eating in Laconnex?*</u>
<u>She ate enough to satisfy her hunger.</u>

<u>*When she left Laconnex, did she take leave of both the wet nurse and her*</u>
   <u>*husband?*</u>
<u>Yes, after eating, she did the accounts with them, and gave them some money.</u>
   <u>When her cousin pressured her to leave, they left together, accompanied by</u>
   <u>the wet nurse to the end of the orchard.</u>

<u>*When they left Laconnex, did they travel along the major roads?*</u>
<u>Yes. They even stopped at the village of Confignon where they took some wine</u>
   <u>and she slept, but her cousin advised her not to stop there for long, though</u>
   <u>they did stay for some time to repair her petticoat.</u>

When they returned to the city, did her cousin immediately leave for Nyon?
Not immediately. Her cousin left her at the door [of her home] in order to
   take care of some business. He then came back to her house where he ate
   something and then left.

What time was it when he left?
She does not remember.

<u>*Did Mademoiselle Fabri ask her if she had gone to Laconnex that day?*</u>
<u>Yes, and she answered "what of it and what has it to do with you?" Whereupon</u>
   <u>Damoiselle Fabri told her that there was some very bad news and that she</u>
   <u>should leave. The deponent asked Damoiselle Fabri for her servant in order</u>
   <u>to return to Laconnex.</u>

<u>*After Damoiselle Fabri spoke to her, did she not make preparations to leave?*</u>

No, she went to the ramparts, but only in order to find a servant named
Pernette who had worked for her before who she had been told had gone to
Longemalle.[17]

Why did she go to the ramparts given that the said Pernette had gone to
Longemalle?
When she goes to Longemalle, she always takes that route, but because she
found the way blocked, she was obliged to retrace her steps and there ran
into the husband of the wet nurse who grabbed her by the arm.

What did the husband of the wet nurse say to her?
He told her that the two children had died and that it was her fault, whereupon
she responded to him that he should not make so much noise and that if he
had anything more to tell her that he should come up to her bedchamber, to
which the said wet nurse's husband replied that she needed to come speak
with an *auditeur*.

How is it possible that the two children were healthy and then suddenly fell ill
with the same sickness without her having contributed to it?
She does not know, but it is possible that one of the children went out and got
something to eat that he gave to the other one since there was a [...] at the
door.
Had she not noticed that the children had cups for drinking?
No.

Did the mother of the wet nurse not bring her a jug of wine and put it on the
hearth?
No.

Had she not put some arsenic into the candies that she fed to the children?
No, God forbid.

Did she not notice that the teeth and tongues of the said children were all black
and that they were very unwell?
No, truly, they were vomiting, but in the end, they quietly fell asleep.

Did her daughter stay sitting on her lap for long?
Once she had finished lacing her up, she put her on her feet.

Was her daughter crying when she was in her lap?

---

[17] Longemalle is a city square located near the Rhone River in the lower city. Walking in the
direction of the Saint-Antoine ramparts was not the most direct route to Longemalle.

No.

Where was her daughter when the wet nurse arrived?
She was sitting on her lap again.

Did she not suggest to the jailer and beg him to release her from prison, and that
she would pay him 1000 écus if he did so?
When she saw the lodgings and was in a very unhappy state, she admits to
having said to the jailer that if he had the power to remove her from there,
she would give him everything that she had in the world.

Summoned to declare that she poisoned the children.
No. God preserve her.

FOLIO 25

[May 14, 1686. Deliberations of the Small Council.]

Friday, May 14, 1686.[18] The entire council present.

Jeanne Thomasset, prisoner. Heard her testimony given in the torture chamber. She was returned [to prison] and will be questioned again
tomorrow.

FOLIO 26

[May 15, 1686. Deliberations of the Small Council.]

Saturday, May 15, 1686.[19] Lieutenant of justice present.

Jeanne Thomasset, prisoner. Having heard her testimony, and in consideration of all the other evidence gathered in the investigation, the council, after praying to God, ordered that today she would be interrogated in
the torture chamber and that, if she continued to deny her guilt, she would
be given one high lift.[20]

---

[18] AEG RC 186, f. 144.
[19] AEG RC 186, f. 144.
[20] One high lift indicates that the council had decided to proceed with the *corde*, a form of
torture.

FOLIO 27

[May 15, 1686. Sixth interrogation of Jeanne Catherine Thomasset, second interrogation in the torture chamber, during which she was subjected to the corde (torture).]

Last Thursday did she not give poison to her daughter and the child of the wet nurse at Laconnex?
No, God help her.

How were they poisoned?
She does not know.

Did she not ask for a cup and some wine from the mother of the wet nurse?
No.

Did she and her cousin de la Fléchère not spend time alone in the kitchen with the two children?
She does not remember.

When she saw the two said children vomiting, did she not fail them by leaving with her said cousin?
No, they finished eating, and, after eating, they settled accounts with the wet nurse.

Why did they make a pretext of leaving promptly due to the supposed illness of her cousin's father and then stop for a long time at Confignon and then again in the city once they returned here?
They stopped at Confignon to repair her torn petticoat and to have a drink.

When Mademoiselle Fabri asked her whether she had been to Laconnex that day, why did she not tell her?
The deponent told her only what suited her because she did not want Damoiselle Fabri to know that she had a child living there.

Summoned again to give glory to God and tell the truth.
She has done so and God knows she is innocent.

After Mademoiselle Fabri spoke to her, did she not start to make preparations to save herself?
No, if she had wanted to save herself, she would not have lingered so long.

When the peasant stopped her, did she not ask him not to say anything?
She told him not to make so much noise and that he should come up to her bedchamber.

Does she not acknowledge having written this letter, produced here and in part read aloud to her? Would she care to comment on its contents?[21]
Yes, it is a letter that she wrote to Sieur Roch in order to have him understand that she would send the child born to her and his brother, which she had always hidden from him, to the Vaud.

Did she and her cousin, either together or separately, cause the death of the two children?
No, she is innocent and God knows it.

If she is innocent of the crime who then is guilty of the said crime, since it necessarily was someone who was in the room?
She does not know and she is not a magician who knows who commits all crimes.

Why did the said de la Fléchère go with her to Laconnex when his father was ill?
She asked him to accompany her in order to help her settle accounts with the wet nurse.

Who is this Pernette whom she claims she went to find on the ramparts?
She lives in Mademoiselle Fabri's house.

Who told her that she had gone to Longemalle?
One of the neighbors, whom she does not know.

Before going to Laconnex, did she not plan to poison her child?
No, God save her.

What is the profession of her cousin de la Fléchère and did he learn these things from a surgeon or from an apothecary?
She does not know.

Right after she gave birth, did she not wish for the death of her child?
She may very well have said that she wished that God would take both herself and her child from this world.

The said Thomasset is attached to the torture instruments.

Did she not give poison to the two children while she was in Laconnex?
No, God knows it.

Did she not give her daughter some wine in a cup?
No.

---

[21] Possibly Folio 12.

Was it her cousin who gave the said wine in the said cup?
She believes him to be a better man than to have committed this crime.

Give glory to God by admitting the truth.
She is innocent. God give her strength. She will whisper nothing against her will.
She is lifted. Said, "My God, have pity on your servant! I never committed this
crime!"[22]

*Lifted higher and commanded to speak the truth. Said again that she was
innocent and beseeched God to fortify her and to send his angels to her.*
Saying, "Alas, my God, my Savior, they torture my body as much as they want,
my soul does not suffer."

Once again summoned to tell the truth. Responded only by sighing.
It was then ordered that she be lowered, which was done, and she was given
some wine in order to fortify her heart. And then exhorted to speak the
truth in order not to be lifted again and tortured. Again, she confirmed her
protestations of innocence.

Was it not her cousin who put the poison into the cup?
It was not her and she does not believe that her cousin did it.

Did she not ask for some wine in the cup?
No.

*She was then detached from the instruments and urged to examine her
conscience.*

FOLIO 28

[May 17, 1686. Deliberations of the Small Council.]

Monday, May 17, 1686.[23] Noble Lect is absent.

Jeanne Catherine Thomasset, prisoner. Regarding her second interrogation in the torture chamber, during which, persisting in her denials
regarding the poisoning of the two children at Laconnex and consistently
insisting on her innocence, she was attached to the torture instruments
and lifted up high. She continued to deny [the accusation], even when she

---

[22] Note the shift from the third person account ("she said") to the first person ("I said") while
pain is applied. This is a direct quotation.
[23] AEG RC 186, f. 145–6.

was lowered to the ground and detached from the instruments, which is to be regretted. Ordered that the interrogation will continue, regardless of her obstinate refusal to confess, and that she will be subjected to the full procedure today at two o'clock.

Later that day.[24]

Jeanne Catherine Thomasset, prisoner. Regarding her third interrogation in the torture chamber during which, before and after torture and even after receiving the "entire torture" [the *estrapade*], she persisted constantly and firmly in denying being guilty of the crime of which we accuse her. Ordered that torture be continued tomorrow and that, in the meantime, a minister be sent to speak with her and she be moved to a different prison cell.

FOLIO 29

[May 17, 1686. Seventh interrogation of Jeanne Catherine Thomasset, third interrogation in the torture chamber, during which she received the estrapade, the most painful form of torture employed in Geneva.]

Summoned to speak the truth about the death of her daughter and that of the child of the wet nurse because the Messieurs would like to know and are prepared to give her a sharp drop of the rope.
God will offer her succor.

Did she not bring some poison, such as arsenic or another drug capable of killing, from the Vaud region or did she buy it elsewhere?
No. God knows this and she never once imagined doing so. One day God will reveal her innocence and will reveal the truth of these events, of which she is entirely innocent.

Did her cousin administer the poison?
She does not know, but she does not believe so since he is incapable of committing such a cruel act. He is a good man.

Did she or her said cousin not give some wine or some drink to these two children?
No, God preserve her.

If it was not by way of the said cup that the said children were poisoned, is it not true that it was by means of the candy that she fed them the poison?

---

[24] After the interrogation in Folio 27.

No. God knows. Why would she have formed a plan to kill these poor children when she had always cared so well for her daughter?

Having been told that her cousin had blamed her,[25] she responded that if this was true, then he had such a black soul that God would never forgive him. Then she said that this [accusation] was false and that she had never thought of killing her child.

Represented to her that she must not refrain from telling the truth by the considerations of this world since she has little chance of being released. Seeing as she is likely to be condemned to death, she must make peace with God by confessing her sins in order to obtain the forgiveness of His Grace.

Responded that they could do whatever they wished to her, but she would not confess to what she had not done. She was innocent of what she was accused of doing.

Attached to the torture instruments.

Urged to confess so as to avoid being tortured.
Said nothing.

Having been lifted a little, asked if it were not true that she committed this crime of poisoning.
Replied God will preserve her.

Summoned again to confess.
Did not respond.

Having been lifted a little higher, and exhorted to give glory to God and confess her crime.
Did not respond.

Having been lifted to all the way to the top, she was told that she would be dropped and she will confess. Was it not true that she poisoned her own child?
No.

After being dropped sharply, asked her if it was not true that she had committed this crime?
Shook her head, no.

---

[25] The interrogators are lying here. See Folio 30.

──────────────── **FOLIO 30** ────────────────

[May 17, 1686. Testimony of nobleman Daniel de la Fléchère, cousin of Jeanne Catherine, who accompanied her to Laconnex the day the children died. This testimony was collected by Noble Nicolas Steiguer, bailiff of Nyon, in Nyon rather than in Geneva. Nyon was a city in the Vaud region in Switzerland, a separate state from the republic of Geneva.]

We, Nicolas Steiguer, bailiff of Nyon, attest to have summoned Noble Daniel François de la Fléchère before us today, the 17th of May 1686, to establish what occurred during his visit to Laconnex on Thursday, 6th day of the current month, in the company of Jeanne Catherine Thomasset. Having been exhorted to tell the truth, he [Daniel] made the following sworn statement:

Firstly, after they left Geneva to go to the aforementioned village, she was never out of his sight, not even in the house of the wet nurse who had been caring for her daughter for a few years. Upon arriving, an old woman took the child out of the crib and brought the child to her. At once, he noticed how much she wanted to kiss the child and that the abdomen of the child was distended, which he believed was caused by worms. Secondly, she gave the child some candy to eat, some of which he had already eaten himself and ate again later, as did the said Thomasset, his cousin, and various other people in the house. After this, the said girl and the son of the wet nurse, to whom she had also given some, developed heartburn, which they at first attributed to the worms with which they surmised the children were infected. But, as it continued, she had them fetch some *orviétan* or *thériaque*, which she had the children take in some wine, she offering it to her daughter and the wet nurse giving it to her son, which induced them to vomit. Thirdly, throughout the visit, he was pressuring her to leave for Geneva because he had to return imperatively to his father in Nyon, who was gravely ill. She seemed distressed to leave her child and insisted that they stay an hour longer than he wanted. Fourthly, when they left, she told the wet nurse to come to Geneva to fetch some powder to give to one of the children, which she believed, according to what she said, would kill the worms, some of which, she claimed she had left with the wet nurse a year ago. They left the children dozing on a bed. Finally, he noticed no changes in either her face or her behavior during all of this time, even in town where he stopped to eat before leaving for Nyon to tend to his father. We have signed and sealed this declaration, at Nyon on the above-mentioned year and day.

Steiguer
May 17, 1686

–––––––––––––––––––– **FOLIO 31** ––––––––––––––––––––

[May 18, 1686. Further testimony of Jeanne Vautier.]

Further testimony of Damoiselle Jeanne Vautier, widow of Noble Urbain Fabri, about sixty years of age, duly taken the oath.

Adding to her previous testimony, the Wednesday night when Jeanne Catherine Thomasset returned from the Vaud region, she told the daughter of the deponent that her eyes were sore and that she thought she would not go out the next day, which the said Thomasset did not adhere to since she went to the village of Laconnex the next day. The deponent also added that when she went to the said Thomasset's room to warn her that there were peasants in the street who were complaining that she had caused the death of two children, one of whom belonged to the said Thomasset, she replied "how dare they say that, that she had behaved very well, that she would go and speak with them." And since the deponent was very surprised by this response, she told the said Thomasset to leave her room and go, in order to avoid the unpleasantness of her being seized in her home by an *auditeur*, whom the peasants had gone to find. The deponent added that she should lock her bedchamber, which the said Damoiselle did, and left, going in the direction of the Boulevard Saint-Antoine where she stayed for some time and then came back and was seized.

The deponent added that when the said Thomasset returned from Laconnex, she went to eat at the shop run by Damoiselle Rey, widow of the minister, who in turn told the deponent the next day that the said Thomasset seemed very sad. When Damoiselle Rey asked the said Thomasset why, she said that her father was still mourning the death of his son and that she was similarly affected. The deponent also added that the brother of the said Thomasset had been sick for some fifteen days at her house and that she had noticed that, before he fell sick, he had a dry cough, a sore neck and a headache, about which he complained, accompanied by vomiting. That she does not know anything more about the circumstances of which she has been questioned.

Repeated, read aloud, witness confirmed testimony, and did not sign because does not know how.

Pan, syndic.

---------------------------- **FOLIO 32** ----------------------------

[May 19, 1686. Eighth interrogation of Jeanne Catherine Thomasset, fourth in the torture chamber. She makes reference to the recent death of her brother Samuel and to the physician, Gabriel Cramer, who cared for him during his last illness.]

Is she not disposed to tell the truth? Does she finally have a contrite heart and a penitent soul?
She cannot go against her conscience.

On the day she returned from the Vaud region to Geneva, did she not say to Mademoiselle Fabri that she had sore eyes and that she would not be going out the next day?
She certainly told her that she had sore eyes, but she does not remember saying that she would not go out the next day and, even if she had said that, this is not evidence against her.

Where did she go after she returned from Laconnex and ate?
Mademoiselle Fabri told her that Mademoiselle Rey had been looking for her, so she went to find her and stayed with her some time.

Why was she upset when she visited with Mademoiselle Rey and was it not because the two children had died?
No, she is totally innocent and she was no more upset than on previous visits.

Did the said Damoiselle Rey not ask her why she was sad and did she not reply that it was because her father was still very upset by the death of her brother?
She does not remember what the said Damoiselle might have said to her, but the deponent could well have spoken about the death of her brother.

Before her brother fell ill, did he have any previous health problems?
He was never the most healthy nor the least healthy, but he did experience headaches.

Did his final illness last a long time and what was the diagnosis?
It lasted fifteen days and Sieur Cramer said that he had blood in his brain and [it is true] that he never complained about anywhere but his head.

Did he not have stomach pains and was his stomach not hard and distended?
She does not know what caused his death, but it could have been because of the quantity of purges that were done and medicine that he had in his body, and then she said: "Alas, my Lord."

Did he not experience severe vomiting?
Yes.

Was his vomiting not similar to that of the two children who died in Laconnex?
Her brother's vomiting was caused by having his stomach opened, as Sieur
    Favre and another woman who examined him both confirmed, and the
    children did not vomit as much.

Did her brother not complain of severe headaches?
No. They perhaps suspected her of having poisoned her brother, but God
    knows she did not and she is also completely innocent of having killed the
    two children.

Who then killed the said children?
She does not know. The child of the wet nurse was not even in the house when
    she arrived, but somewhere in the village.

*Did she not poison the said children, either by mixing poison in some wine or in
    the candy or otherwise?*
No, and she will never confess to something she has not done.

Summoned to tell the truth in order to avoid the torments that are prepared for her.
When she was made to suffer on two other occasions, they could nevertheless
    not make her admit to what she had not done.

*She was told that she could die during the torments and, if this occurred, she
    would be eternally damned.*
She replied that she ardently wished to die, and that God would send angels to
    take her soul to paradise. Reiterated that she was completely innocent.

Did she not say that the children had poisoned themselves?
Replied that the child of the wet nurse, who was outside the house, could have
    brought something poisonous back with him.

Attached to the torture instruments.

*Exhorted, urged, and summoned to tell the truth of her crime, whether she
    poisoned her child either by the cup or with the candy or in some other way?*
She is innocent and she cannot respond and do wrong by confessing what
    she has never done. It was possible that the child of the wet nurse, who was
    outside the house, could have brought something in that he might have given
    to her daughter. They ought to speak again with those who accuse her before
    causing so much suffering.

Lifted and summoned to tell the truth.
Replied that she has done so, and that she has repeated it three different times,
    and said "Alas, my Lord, come to my aid."

Was subjected to an abrupt drop.

After a short pause, was exhorted to tell the truth, that she poisoned her child.
She made a sign with her head indicating no.

--------------------------------- **FOLIO 33** ---------------------------------

[May 22, 1686. Deliberations of the Small Council.]

Saturday, May 22, 1686.[26] Nobles Lect, Humbert, and Franconis absent.
Monsieur the Lieutenant present.
    Laconnex. Heard a report that Sieur de la Place has sent a request to the
husband of the wet nurse, father of the dead boy, and another subject living in the village of Avully possibly with the intention of questioning them
further regarding this matter. Requesting instructions regarding how to
proceed. Told that they were not to go there [to Laconnex] and that if there
is any sign of anyone having done so, report back immediately.
    Later the same day.[27] Daniel de la Fléchère de Nyon. The council debated
whether to charge de la Fléchère. Decided not to do so. Further deliberation
regarding what to do with the prisoner Thomasset. It was proposed that she
be shaved and that she be confronted once again with the wet nurse and the
husband of the wet nurse. It was decided that the head and armpits of the
said Thomasset would be shaved. Secondly, that the said individuals [wet
nurse and husband of the wet nurse] would not be summoned to court.

--------------------------------- **FOLIO 34** ---------------------------------

*[Undated letter, probably written May 24, 1686, by the father of Jeanne Cath-
erine, Jean François Thomasset, and other male relatives. These relatives
included several male cousins, including the Roch brothers who were likely
closely related to the father of her child.]*

Magnificent and very honored Lords,

We, Noble Jean François Thomasset together with Noble Jean Pierre Thomasset, seigneur of Crose; Jacques François and Samuel Thomasset, the seigneur of Rosey; Sieur Roch, lawyer, and his brothers; Sieur Banderot, mayor

---

[26] AEG RC 186, f. 148.
[27] AEG RC 186, f. 149.

of Morges; Sieur Jean Pierre Christin of Orbe; and Étienne Vallotton, *châtelain* [of Vallorbe], your own very humble servants.

Addressing ourselves humbly to Your Lords, we set out that Damoiselle Jeanne Catherine Thomasset, his daughter and their kin, having had the misfortune to meet with the honorable Abraham Clerc at his house in Laconnex the day that her daughter and the son of the said Clerc died, and the said Clerc having alleged that poison was the cause, the said Clerc brought her to the criminal prosecutor in this city and accused her of having killed the children by poison.

It pleased Your Lords to imprison the said Thomasset, to collect all information possible regarding the events, and to question her on several occasions regarding the accusation and other matters. We the undersigned consider that none of the evidence necessarily disproves the innocence of the said Thomasset, and indeed it can be considered misleading given that some elements have not been clearly established. It pleased Your Lords to torture the said Thomasset three times in order to extract a confession regarding whether she had committed the crime.

We the undersigned did not lodge a complaint against the use of torture, approved by Your Lords, notwithstanding the weakness of the evidence and the limited extent of proof. The atrocity of the crime could well explain why Your Lords risked the suffering of an innocent woman, using all legal means available to discover whether she had committed the crime.

At present, however, the investigation is entirely complete, Your Lords having now heard the said Thomasset speak about the crime several times and having tried to extract a confession of guilt and other insights from her under torture on as many occasions as the law permits, given the evidence presented in the case. Thus there remains nothing left to do since Your Lords cannot hope to discover new evidence, or any proof, against the said Thomasset.

We the undersigned, who have patiently supported all the procedures it pleased Your Lords to order with the aim of discovering her guilt, even though a guilty conviction against her would have been an affront to us. We are now obliged to appeal to Your Lords' sense of what is right. We request that you repair the shame that this accusation has brought upon our house and beseech Your Lords, given the feeble evidence against her, which has been purged by her denials under torture, particularly because she has suffered, to consider liberating her from prison and declaring her innocent of the crime of which she has been accused by the said Clerc.

In obtaining justice from Your Lords, the undersigned will have all the more reason to pray to God for your prosperity and affirm our devotion to your service.

Étienne Vallotton, J.P. Christin
Signed on behalf of the kin who have withdrawn [left the city].

——————————— **FOLIO 35** ———————————

[May 24, 1686. Letter from the bailiff of Nyon, Nicolas Steiguer, addressed to the Small Council. The document is damaged and difficult to follow. Words that cannot be read are indicated by [...].]

To the illustrious, magnificent, sovereign Lords, good neighbors, singular friends, allies, and confederates,

Since I know that the detention of the Damoiselle, about whom I have already had the honor of writing to Your Lords, has caused you much trouble, and that you would have very much wished that she had fallen into the arms of another court, I believe also that Your Lords have some joy in seeing that after having satisfied everything [...] Your Lords believed [...] matter of condemning her [...] to have for a family of considerable [...] on my part I confess that I take much [...] with pleasure that it is all done with [...] that I hold myself [...] receiving from Your Lords my [...] on the occasion of their [...].

——————————— **FOLIO 36** ———————————

[May 24, 1686. Deliberations of the Small Council.]

Monday, May 24, 1686.[28] Nobles Humbert and Franconis absent today.

Jeanne Catherine Thomasset. In light of the request made by Sieur Thomasset, her father, and other relatives to free her and taking into consideration her most recent testimony given in the torture chamber and the council chamber, after praying to God, considered what there is still to do and whether the investigation is in fact closed. Ordered that we will go to the prison in the afternoon, after she has been shaved, to attach her to the torture instruments, place her on the platform surrounded by instruments of torture, without lifting her.

The Lords of Bern. In consideration of their letter dated the 24th of this month, in which they ask us to interrogate the said Thomasset whether their subject, a man named Roch, with whom she had this incestuous child, was complicit in these crimes and to inform them of the result. Decided that she would be interrogated about him and that sworn testimony would be sought from Sieur Cramer, physician, Sieur Roy, apothecary, and Sieur

---

[28] AEG RC 186, f. 150.

Noël, coroner, regarding the death of the named Thomasset, brother of the prisoner.

──────────────────── FOLIO 37 ────────────────────

[May 24, 1686. Report of the physicians Le Clerc and Beddevole regarding the powder found in the corpses of the two children.]

We, the undersigned physicians, certify and attest to having completed an examination and verification of the powder found in the stomach of the son of [blank] of the village of Laconnex, which we conserved in order to analyze in the following manner.[29]

Firstly, on the tenth of May, we took some flakes of arsenic and combined them with a small amount of potassium carbonate and left it for a fairly long time without observing any change in color. Then, having placed a small amount of mercuric chloride in another container, we similarly combined it with a few drops of potassium carbonate and found that the mixture became a vibrant yellow color. Finally, in a third container, we put approximately the same amount of arsenic and mercuric chloride as we had used in the previous experiments mixed together. We again added potassium carbonate and in a short time everything turned black. Having completed this first experiment, the next day we took some of the heavy material we had found in the stomach of the boy, as we previously indicated in our earlier report, but separated it from the sack in which it was found, noting that it now appeared more white in color than it had when we opened his body. Having dried this powder, we added an equal quantity of mercuric chloride and potassium chloride and watched as this mixture blackened in a matter of moments, as had occurred in the first experiment when we combined both arsenic and mercuric chloride.

Due to these results, combined with the signs of a corrosive poison resulting in inflammation, ulceration of body parts, and other symptoms indicated in our report, we have concluded that the said powder was arsenic. With regard to the powder found in the body of the little girl, we found

---

[29] This test was an established means of verifying poisons in late seventeenth-century Geneva and was considered reliable at the time. Another trial in which the same procedure was used is AEG Procès Criminels 1e Série 5218.

too little to be able to undertake the same experiment. Such is our report, in witness thereof, we have both signed.

Geneva, May 24, 1686
Le Clerc, physician
Beddevole, physician

FOLIO 38

[Undated invoice of the two surgeons.]

Owed to Étienne Demonthoux and Étienne Dentand, master surgeons, for having gone by order of Monsieur the Syndic Pan to Laconnex and spent the entire day there in order to examine and do all that was necessary to verify the poisoning of two children.

For having examined the boy in all the exterior parts of his body. For having examined and studied his mouth, tongue, gums, palate and throat. For having examined and studied all interior parts of his thorax and digestive system.

For having done for the girl the same as for the boy, in addition for the removal of hair, in addition for the reports produced and the oaths taken.

In addition, for having removed a vial of material in order to conduct an experiment that you find attached and by order of the lieutenant of justice.

For all of this work and time spent, each is owed the sum of ten *écus*.

E. Demonthoux
E. Dentand

FOLIO 39

[Undated physicians' invoice for examining corpses.]

Owed to Daniel Le Clerc and to Dominique Beddevole, physicians, for having gone to the village of Laconnex, by the order of the Lords, the 7th of May this year.

Firstly, to compensate them for the journey: one *pistole* each or seventy-seven *florins*.

For having the bodies of the corpses of the poisoned children opened in their presence: one *pistole* each or seventy-seven *florins*.

For the report they wrote jointly with the master surgeons regarding what they found in the corpses of the children, two *écus* or forty-two *florins*.

For the second report they wrote a few days later concerning the nature of the poison and to cover the costs of the experiments done regarding the poison, sixty *florins*.

For the renting of two horses, seven *florins*.

263 *florins*

Le Clerc, physician
Beddevole, physician

FOLIO 40

[May 24, 1686. Ninth interrogation of Jeanne Catherine Thomasset, fifth in the torture chamber.]

Does she not finally want to tell the truth?
She has done so.

Did she not give birth to a child?
Yes.

<u>With whom?</u>
<u>Her cousin Jonas Roch.</u>

<u>Did she not kill her said child?</u>
<u>No, and if her cousin accuses her, he does her wrong and if he did it, he did it</u>
   <u>alone, and she knew nothing about it.</u>

<u>To whom was she referring when she said that God only knows who is responsible</u>
   <u>for this crime?</u>
<u>She cannot say with certainty, but it could have been those people who</u>
   <u>contracted to give her what they had promised with regard to the child.</u>
   Because in making that promise they extracted a counter-promise from her
   that the matter would remain secret, unless the child died, at which point the
   promise was rendered null and void.

<u>Did her cousin de la Fléchère poison the children?</u>
<u>She does not know.</u>

<u>Summoned to tell the truth since her guilt is sufficiently proven.</u>
<u>She is completely innocent and, in any case, someone told her that her cousin</u>
   <u>had admitted that he alone is guilty.</u>

*Once again, if she herself did not poison the children, how is it that she could
know who poisoned them?*

She does not know, but she very much wishes that one speak again to her
accusers to find out whether it is true that the child of the wet nurse, who
had been out in the village, brought something back in his hand that he
perhaps shared with her daughter.

What did he have in his hand?

She does not know, but he let go of it when he took the candy that she gave him
and his mother told him to pick it up.

*Did her cousin remain in the kitchen the entire time or did he go out while the wet
nurse was being called?*

She did not see him leave.

Summoned to give glory to God by admitting her crime.

She has declared her innocence. She thinks it could have been the Roch family,
in order to free themselves of the promise they made her to pay her a sum
[of money] by the feast of Saint John. They delayed the payment, first to
September, then to October of last year, when they should have paid her 200
écus in lieu of the 1000 *écus* they had promised. She does not think she does
them an injustice by arriving at this conclusion.

─────────────────────── **FOLIO 41** ───────────────────────

*[May 24, 1686. Testimony of Sieur Benjamin Noël, coroner, Étienne Demon-
thoux, master surgeon, and Pierre Roy, master apothecary, regarding the
death of Samuel Thomasset, brother of Jeanne Catherine. This information
was gathered by Jean Robert Choüet, professor of science and member of
the Small Council in charge of the prisons. The death of Samuel Thomasset
occurred on March 24, 1686, six weeks before the trial against Jeanne Catherine was initiated.]*

May 24, 1686

Declaration of Sieur Benjamin Noël, received by the noble councillors,
by the syndic and by Choüet the Elder, as a result of a ruling of the Small
Council on this day.

Has declared that on the 24th of March this year, he examined the corpse
of Noble Samuel Thomasset, in the house situated at the Place Bourg-
de-Four belonging to Damoiselle Vautier, widow of Noble Urbain Fabri.

He recalled and also verified with reference to his registry, that he [Samuel] died of apoplexy,[30] having reached this conclusion as a result of the jugular veins being extremely swollen. Did not see any sign or indication that the said Thomasset had died of poison. Had remarked that his abdomen was very hard, the flesh of the body firm and solid. Swore an oath to this effect, and does not know anything more.

Repeated, read aloud, witness confirmed testimony, and signed.

B. Noël, coroner
Pan, syndic
R. Choüet

———

I, undersigned, master surgeon, certify that after having taken an oath administered by Monsieur the Syndic Pan, that I tended Monsieur Samuel Thomasset in his final illness of which he died the 24th of March, 1686. Declared having bled him twice, once in the foot and the other time in the arm accompanied by cupping. The first bleeding was in the foot. The day preceding it, he experienced convulsions, the abdomen was very hard and extended. He was very tormented and agitated from the convulsions, without again regaining the power of speech during this illness, and all the remedies, both internal and external, did not in any way relieve his suffering.

In witness thereof, signed May 24, 1686.

Étienne Demonthoux
Pan, syndic
R. Choüet

———

I, undersigned, master apothecary, certify, after having taken the oath administered by Monsieur the Syndic Pan, that I provided the medicines ordered by Monsieur Cramer, physician, for Sieur Samuel Thomasset who died the 24th of March, 1686 of continual convulsions, which lasted twenty-four hours, during which no remedy was effective, not emetics, not purgatives, nor bleeding or cupping. The abdomen was so hard and distended that even hot compresses and enemas had no effect and he lost

---

[30] Cerebral hemorrhage or a stroke.

the power of speech once the sickness overtook him. Having nothing more to report, I signed.

May 24, 1686
Pierre Roy, apothecary
Pan, syndic
R. Choüet

─────────────── **FOLIO 42** ───────────────

[May 25, 1686. Deliberations of the Small Council.]

Tuesday May 25, 1686.[31] Noble Franconis absent and Monsieur the Lieutenant present.

The Lords of Bern. Examined and approved the letter received from these lords regarding the criminal prosecution of their subject Jeanne Catherine Thomasset, imprisoned in Geneva.

─────────────── **FOLIO 43** ───────────────

[May 26, 1686. Deliberations of the Small Council.]

Wednesday May 26, 1686.[32] Nobles Humbert and Franconis absent and Monsieur the Lieutenant present.

Jeanne Catherine Thomasset, prisoner. Regarding her most recent testimony given in the torture chamber, the council decided that a final sentence in the trial should be issued within eight days.

─────────────── **FOLIO 44** ───────────────

[May 28, 1686. Letter written by Jean François Thomasset and other male relatives.]

───────────

[31] AEG RC 186, f. 151.
[32] AEG RC 186, f. 152.

Magnificent and very honored Lords,

Noble Jean François Thomasset; Noble Jean Pierre Thomasset, seigneur of Crose; Jacques François and Samuel Thomasset; Noble Laurent Quisart, seigneur of Rosey; Noble Jean Gabriel Mayor, *banderet* of Morges; Sieur Roch, lawyer, and his brothers; Sieur Margel, minister of Bullet; Jean Pierre Christin of Orbe; Étienne Vallotton, *châtelain* of Vallorbe and generally all the kin of the said Noble Jean François Thomasset, your very humble servants.

We humbly addressed, on Monday 24th day of the present month, a request to Your Lords that Damoiselle Jeanne Catherine Thomasset be freed and be declared innocent, since, as a result of her replies and her suffering, all evidence that has been amassed against her has been purged, all information that can be gathered has been gathered, and nothing remains to be done.

Given that this letter has neither been acknowledged nor responded to on the part of Your Lords, the undersigned find themselves obliged to make a further appeal that Your Lords reconsider the contents of the said request and, in order to relieve the supplicants of the distress to which the accusations made against the said Damoiselle Thomasset have subjected them, console them and bring an end to the disadvantageous and dishonorable talk to which she has exposed them.

May it please Your Lords to provide what is required and concede the terms and desired outcomes of this request.

In the meantime, the undersigned continue to pray to God for the prosperity of Your Lords.

> Jean François Thomasset in the name of all his kin
> J.P. Christin; J. Margel, son-in-law; Étienne Vallotton

FOLIO 45

[May 28, 1686. Deliberations of the Small Council.]

Friday May 28, 1686.[33] Noble Humbert absent today.

Jeanne Catherine Thomasset. Regarding the report presented by Monsieur the Mayor about a request from her relatives and a letter from the

---

[33] AEG RC 186, f. 153.

Lord Bailiff of Nyon. [The council] should examine whether it is appropriate to proceed to a judgment [now], or whether to reconvene next Wednesday, which is the eighth day, as was previously decided. Decided to adhere to the former resolution.

FOLIO 46

[June 2, 1686. Letter addressed to the mayor of Geneva written by Romier Laisné, a relative of the Thomassets, on behalf of Jeanne Catherine. The manuscript is somewhat damaged.]

Very honorable and magnificent Lord,

The goodness and lack of a perfect sympathy that I experienced in recent days from Your Lords [...] the liberty to offer very humbly my view that the requests presented to Your Lords on the 24th and 28th of the month of May, by your very humble servants, be fulfilled.[34] Together all the kin of Damoiselle Jeanne Catherine Thomasset continue to request that it please Your Lords to liberate and declare innocent the said Thomasset. Since her guilt is not proven by any form of evidence, nor has she confessed, and she has withstood and maintained [her innocence] through all procedures that your laws require and, in so doing, she has been completely and entirely purged of the charges laid against her. Since there remains no further legal procedure to undertake, I once again very humbly beseech Your Lords to console all of us by relieving us of the disgrace to which we have been exposed.

I appeal to the grace and mercy of Your Lords, to whom I am entirely, in general and in every particular, your very humble and very obedient servant.

Romier Laisné
Yverdon
June 2, 1686

---

[34] Here Romier Laisné makes reference to the two letters sent by Jean François Thomasset and other relatives requesting Jeanne Catherine's release. See Folios 34 and 44.

─────────────── **FOLIO 47** ───────────────

[July 5, 1686. Deliberations of the Small Council. The last deliberations regarding Jeanne Catherine had occurred on May 28, five weeks earlier.]

Monday, July 5, 1686.[35] Noble Jacques Pictet, syndic, and Noble Lect absent.

Jeanne Catherine Thomasset, prisoner and defendant for the crime of poisoning. The council gathered to render judgment on her case. Praying to God, having read the legal protocol, the surgeons' report, and the testimony submitted, [the council] decided to rule on the matter tomorrow.

─────────────── **FOLIO 48** ───────────────

[July 16, 1686. Summary of the arguments of the prosecution.]

Criminal trial undertaken and pursued before our magnificent and very honored Lords, syndics and council of this city at the instigation and under the authority of the Lord Lieutenant in this instance against Jeanne Catherine Thomasset of Orbe in Switzerland.

She, having been taken prisoner, has been sufficiently proven to have, on the sixth day of the month of May last, gone in the early morning to the village of Laconnex with a relative, named in the trial, in order to visit her child, conceived in debauchery, whom she arranged to have nursed there secretly for the past two years.

Moreover, having only found the mother of the wet nurse in the house, the said Thomasset told her to get her child out of the crib, and then, having taken the said child, who was perfectly healthy, onto her lap, she told the woman to go and call the wet nurse who was at the fountain.

Moreover, the said Thomasset and her kin having been left alone in the house, the said wet nurse and her mother returned seven or eight minutes later. Moments after, the said child and the child of the wet nurse, who was five years old and in good health, began to vomit, frequently and violently, and soon after experienced convulsions and fainting.

Moreover, the said Thomasset, instead of remaining near her child in order to care for her in the poor state in which she found her, instead left with her said relative.

---

[35] AEG RC 186, f. 180.

Moreover, once they left, the said children, suffering continual and violent convulsions, were taken by death, one after the other, two or three hours later, showing every sign and symptom of a veritable poisoning. This became evident when the expert physicians and surgeons autopsied their corpses in which they conclusively discovered arsenic, as well as various other circumstances and convincing evidence, that preceded, accompanied, and followed the said crime, more amply described in the trial.

───────────────── **FOLIO 49** ─────────────────

[July 18, 1686. Letter written by Romier Laisné addressed to the mayor of Geneva.]

Monsieur,

We, the closest relatives of Damoiselle Thomasset and myself, beseech you very humbly, with the good reputation and influence of our family in mind, to have it please the Small Council to assure the honor of her family and all the rest of the lineage, by liberating this miserable woman while preserving both law and conscience. With regards to the costs [of the trial], whatever they are and for whatever reason they might have come about, if the Small Council does not have the means to pay for these expenses, they [the family] will cover them. I hope that you will do me the favor of satisfying the request that we are making of you, and give us your reply, for which we would be eternally grateful. I offer Your Lords my deep respect, as do the kinsmen whom I represent.

Your very humble and very obedient servant,
Romier Laisné
Cossonay
July 18, 1686

───────────────── **FOLIO 50** ─────────────────

[July 20, 1686. Deliberations of the Small Council.]

Monday, July 20, 1686.[36] Noble Lect absent. Lieutenant of justice present.

───────────

[36] AEG RC 186, f. 189.

Nous Pasteurs soussignés commis par la Vener.
Compagnie, pour exhorter et consoler Jeanne
Catherine Thomasse condannée à la mort par
arrest de Nos Seigneurs, et pour la conduire depuis
les prisons jusques au lieu du supplice. Attestons
qu'en sortant de la prison elle parut fort surprise
de veoir dans la rue une grande foule de peuple
qui l'attendoit pour la veoir en passant, et qu'elle
dit en s'arrestant, esce qu'on me veut produire
aux yeux de tout ce peuple.

Item qu'après avoir ouy la lecture de sa sentence, elle dit
Esce qu'on ne pourroit pas changer ce supplice en une
prison perpetuelle, se croyoy qu'on m'es condanneroit
a une prison perpetuelle.

Item qu'estant au dessus de la descente de la treille, d'ou
on comenceoit a veoir le lieu du supplice, elle n'osa
parler de son Innocence et comença a prier Dieu aue
plus de zele, qu'il luy pardonnast tous ses peches.

Item qu'en s'en passant plus tost, elle dit qu'elle souhaitoit, qu'on
luy accordast de graces, que son corps après sa mort
ne fust pas enterré sous le gibet, et qu'alors on
prit occasion de luy dire, que le Magistrat en
consideration de ses parents auroit favorisé deux
trois choses, la 1re qu'elle ne seroit ni liée ni saisie
par le bourreau qui marchoit à quelques pas,
d'elle ce on le luy fit remarquer, la 2de

Excerpt from the Report of the Ministers, July 27, 1686
CH AEG P.C. 1e série 4694.

Jeanne Catherine Thomasset, prisoner accused of poisoning. After a prayer to God, the council proceeded to judge the case. Considering her guilt sufficiently proven by means of the amassed and accumulated evidence, whose truth cannot be disputed, the council condemns the said Thomasset to death by a first vote, confirmed by a second vote. The form of punishment will be beheading at Plainpalais, as is the custom, with confiscation of her goods to the state.

FOLIO 51

[July 23, 1686. Deliberations of the Small Council.]

Friday, July 23, 1686.[37] Nobles de la Rive, de Normandie, Lect absent.

Jeanne Catherine Thomasset. Represented that it is necessary to send ministers to the prisoner in order to urge her [to confess] given her obstinate refusal to do so, before the day of her execution. Ordered Noble Jean Robert Choüet, the councillor responsible for the prisons, to have a minister visit her today, tomorrow, and Sunday. The execution is scheduled for Monday.

FOLIO 52

[Late July 1686. Letter from Jean François Thomasset requesting mercy for Jeanne Catherine.]

Magnificent and very honored Lords,

It is with keen regret that Noble Jean François Thomasset and all his kinsmen, your humble servants, have learned of the death sentence that it has pleased Your Lords to render against Damoiselle Jeanne Catherine Thomasset, his daughter and their kinswoman, for the crime for which she has been accused. As Your Lords do nothing without careful consideration and given that charity reigns supreme in the council, the said Thomasset and his kinsmen humbly beseech Your Lords to cultivate the initial stirrings of your charity, begging you please, to lighten the public sentence that you have issued, by permitting instead a punishment behind closed doors in the prison.

---

[37] AEG RC 186, f. 191.

With this act of mercy and other particulars, Your Lords will incur a debt of gratitude from a large family.

Continuing to pray to God for your estate and for the illustrious personages that serve it,

Thomasset

FOLIO 53

[July 23–4, 1686. Four letters exchanged between the bailiff of Nyon, Nicolas Steiguer, and the Small Council of Geneva.]

Illustrious, magnificent, sovereign Lords, our dear neighbors, allies and confederates,

I take it upon myself to write to Your Lords regarding the criminal trial of your prisoner whom I have heard was condemned last Tuesday, against the expectation of the entire country. I thought it right to beg you, in fulfilling the sentence, to preserve [the reputation of] such a large number of gentlemen, and have her executed in the prison. I believe that Your Lords would be right to set aside custom, given the present situation and considering how important it would be not to alienate the spirits of almost all of the officers in the country, who are very much interested in this event. It is important to accommodate them to some degree. They have entrusted their request with me, and I found this intercession to be so just and so necessary that I did not hesitate to agree to it immediately. I thus very much hope, having written you already on three occasions, without receiving any satisfaction, that Your Lords would not have me believe, by refusing again, that they [our requests] are considered unimportant among those that I make. For as one knows, it does not seem too much to ask to acquiesce to something that in no way injures one's conscience.

Nevertheless I will never cease to be, illustrious, magnificent, sovereign Lords, Messieurs the Syndics and the council of the Republic of Geneva, our dear neighbors, allies, and confederates, your very humble and obedient servant.

N. Steiguer
Nyon
July 23, 1686

Noble Prince, Bailiff of Nyon,

We have received the letters that it pleased you to offer us regarding the subject of the said Thomasset. We are very sympathetic to your interest in her case and we take it upon ourselves to communicate the esteem with which we view your recommendation. Given the current state of affairs and in view of how we are able to take into consideration your request and the request made by so honorable a family, we have decided to change the ordinary punishment[38] to that of simple decapitation. Praying, Monsieur, to continue to be worthy of the affection that we continue to extend to you,

[unsigned]

———

Noble magnificent, powerful and very honorable Lords, good friends and neighbors, treasured allies and confederates,

Since the Thomasset affair affects several persons of quality in this country, I have already taken the liberty to write to you upon the subject. And I find myself again obliged, on their behalf, to reiterate to you the same request that I have made to you in my previous letters. Rest assured that I will ever remain yours truly, most noble, magnificent, powerful and very honorable Lords,
    Your very humble and very obedient servant,

N. Steiguer
July 24, 1686

———

July 24, 1686

Your Lord, Bailiff of Nyon,

Yesterday we received the letter that it pleased you to send us regarding the fate of the prisoner, and we conclude that at the same time our own letter,

---

[38] The ordinary punishment for infanticide and poisoning was, by the late seventeenth century, death by hanging. By changing her punishment from hanging to decapitation, the council was taking into consideration the fact that Jeanne Catherine was a noblewoman.

addressed to you, will have now been delivered by the messenger. We have most certainly taken into consideration your letter and the attached request made by the family, but, Monsieur, we have not been able to accommodate you as you wished, since what you suggest is a novelty that would result in too many consequences.[39] Nevertheless, in order to prove to you that we undertake this process with the utmost mildness and in a spirit of mitigation, we have resolved to distinguish her from other criminals by having her buried in a different location from other criminals and not to bind her while traveling to the place of execution.

We reiterate, Monsieur, as we have on other occasions, the esteem in which we hold you.

[unsigned]

FOLIO 54

[July 24, 1686. Deliberations of the Small Council.]

Saturday, July 24, 1686.[40] Nobles de la Rive, Grenus, Lect absent. Lieutenant of justice present.

Lord Bailiff of Nyon and Noble Jean François Thomasset. Regarding the third letter written in favor of Jeanne Catherine Thomasset to which the council has not yet responded, he [her father] requests that, in consideration of himself and of his many relatives of high estate from a state that is allied [to Geneva], some of whom are officers in this jurisdiction, that we execute her secretly, in the prison. The contents of this letter, written by her father and other relatives, were debated and it was decided that this request could not be fulfilled. The sentence will be undertaken as ordered, with the exception that she will not be bound with rope on the way to execution and that, in lieu of putting her body on display at the execution site in Champel, her body will be buried behind the *cives*. Ordered that a letter be written to the Lord Bailiff. This letter has been read and approved.

---

[39] The novelty proposed was that Jeanne Catherine be punished in the prison behind closed doors rather than in public.
[40] AEG RC 186, f. 192.

--------------------------- **FOLIO 55** ---------------------------

[July 26, 1686. Final sentence issued against Jeanne Catherine Thomasset. The original manuscript is damaged.]

My very honored Lords, having seen the criminal trial prosecuted and completed before you at the behest and authority of the Lord Lieutenant, the said charges against Jeanne Catherine Thomasset by which their [...] sufficiently [...] without any fear of God she heedlessly poisoned her child and the child [of the] wet nurse, whose deaths followed closely one upon the other, [the] circumstance and crime meriting severe corporal punishment.

[...] seated in the tribunal, in the place of their ancestors, following their ancient customs, having God and His Sacred Writings before their eyes and invoking his Holy Name, in order to render a righteous judgment, in the Name of the Father, the Son, and the Holy Ghost, Amen.

By this, their final sentence, which they give here in writing, condemns Damoiselle Thomasset, as punishment for the said crime, to be led to Plainpalais to be beheaded on the scaffold and so to end her days in order to serve as an example to all who might be tempted to commit such a crime. Declaring in addition her goods be acquired and devolve to the Small Council. Mandating the Lord Lieutenant to execute the present sentence.

--------------------------- **FOLIO 56** ---------------------------

[July 26, 1686. Deliberations of the Small Council. The council consulted with Louis Tronchin, a well-respected minister, professor of theology, and former president of the theological academy of Geneva. The council also consulted with an apothecary, Sieur Visembue, who was suspected of having sold poison to Jeanne Catherine.]

Monday, July 26, 1686.[41] Nobles de la Rive, Lect absent. Lieutenant of justice present.

Jeanne Catherine Thomasset, prisoner for the crime of poisoning. Examined her criminal trial and sentence and they have been confirmed.

---

[41] AEG RC 186, f. 193.

Immediately afterwards, the respected Louis Tronchin, minister, having entered with permission, reported that he had been with the prisoner in order to prepare her for her death and that it seemed that, while at prayer, she was much distressed, but that, in the end, she remained constant in her stubbornness.

After this, Sieur Visembue and his journeyman, called before the court to testify, reported that a young woman, named here, visited his shop some six weeks ago asking for arsenic. When asked if the said young woman was the prisoner and whether he would be able to recognize her, he said that he did not think he would be able to do so.

It was again reported that gossip is circulating that the prisoner might be abducted, which is to be feared given that she has a large and considerable family. Ordered as a precaution a dozen soldiers, half of them armed with muskets, half of them armed with halbards, to accompany Thomasset [to the place of execution]. The sentence was executed today.

──────────────── **FOLIO 57** ────────────────

[July 26, 1686. Report of Auditeur Perdriau. Pierre Perdriau was a thirty-year-old citizen of Geneva and had previously served as auditeur in 1683. In this report, he makes reference to confessions made by Jeanne Catherine to two well-respected men in Geneva whose word would have been trusted by the community. François Turretini, sixty-two years old and a member of the Italian community of Geneva, was a professor of theology and former principal of the Genevan Academy. Antoine Léger was a professor of philosophy and natural sciences at the Genevan Academy.]

I, the undersigned *auditeur*, certify that Our Lords having given me the order that today, between ten and eleven o'clock in the morning, the sentence rendered by them against Jeanne Catherine Thomasset of Orbe in Switzerland, condemned to death for the crime of poisoning, be executed, I accompanied her to Plainpalais. Having been notified that, as she mounted the ladder, she wished to speak to the noble and respected professor of theology François Turretini, I had him summoned and therein he met us at the entrance to Plainpalais. I noticed that the said Thomasset showed much satisfaction at seeing him. It was then reported that she confessed to her crime, which obliged me to get off my horse and approach the said Thomasset in order to learn the truth from her own mouth. Having asked her if it was not true that she had poisoned her daughter and the son of the wet nurse's husband, named during the trial, she whispered to me: "It is true."

I then questioned her about the manner of this poisoning, but since she did not respond, the respected minister and professor of philosophy, Antoine Léger, who had heard her former statement, spoke up and said that she had mixed some poison into the candy. She had only given it to her own child, but the wet nurse's child had snatched the candy into his own hands and had eaten it. Whereupon the said Thomasset, continuing to whisper, said, "That is how it happened." Having summoned her again to declare the details of what had occurred herself, I could draw no response from her, she was so overwhelmed and confused, other than, "That is what happened with the candy." The said Thomasset made this confession at the foot of the scaffold in the presence of a multitude of people, both from the city and from abroad. Among others, I recognized around me the respected Melchisédec Pinault; Antoine Léger, who had accompanied her to the place of execution to console her; the respected Bernard, minister of Saconnex; Dacier, minister of Vandoeuvres; Sarazin, minister of Ventoux; Jérémie Pictet, minister; Du Toict, minister of Vicques in Switzerland; Jean Ulrich Blas, minister of Zurich; the Noble Jacques Gautier, *auditeur*; Daniel Chabrey, acting master of the keys; Robert Rilliet and Abraham Mestrezat, former *auditeurs*; Sieur Jacques Dunant the Younger; Jean Roua; Sieur [blank] Goguin, and Sieur Jean Pierre Charton.

The said Thomasset, then having mounted the scaffold, declared herself guilty of the said crime of poisoning in a loud and intelligible voice. She asked forgiveness of God and of Justice and [declared] that she had been justly condemned.

Vouching with my faith for all that I have drawn up in this report, which I have written and signed by my hand in Geneva this twenty-sixth day of July, sixteen hundred eighty-six.

Perdriau, auditeur
D. Chabrey, acting master of the keys

FOLIO 58

[July 27, 1686. Deliberations of the Small Council.]

Tuesday, July 27, 1686.[42] Nobles de la Rive, Rocca, Lect, Humbert absent. Monsieur the Lieutenant present.

---

[42] AEG RC 186, f. 194–5.

Jeanne Catherine Thomasset. It has been reported by Monsieur the Mayor that yesterday, before her execution, she confessed [her guilt] to some pastors and to *Auditeur* Sieur Perdriau, who presided over the said justice and execution. [She confessed] that she had poisoned the girl with some candy blended with arsenic and that the son of the wet nurse had grabbed a piece from her said daughter. Ordered that they submit their reports to the court.

FOLIO 59

[July 27, 1686. Report of the ministers who heard the final confession of Jeanne Catherine. The original manuscript is damaged.]

We the undersigned ministers, charged by the Venerable Company [of Pastors of Geneva], to exhort and console Jeanne Catherine Thomasset, condemned to death by the judgment of Our Lords, and to accompany her from the jail to the place of punishment. We attest that upon leaving the jail, she seemed very surprised to see the large crowd of people waiting to watch as we passed. Stopping, she asked, "Do they want me to go forth in front of all these people?"

Moreover, after having heard the reading of the sentence, she asked, "Will they not change the sentence to perpetual imprisonment? I believed that they would condemn me to perpetual imprisonment!"

Moreover, as we neared the place of execution and could see the platform, she ceased to talk about her innocence, and began to pray to God with more fervor that He would pardon her for all her sins.

Moreover, a little bit later, she said that she hoped that we would afford her some grace, that after death her body would not be buried under the scaffold. We then took the opportunity to tell her that the council, in consideration of her family's rank, had granted her three things: the first being that she would be neither bound nor seized by the executioner, who we pointed out was walking a few steps away from her; the second being that she would be neither strangled nor burned, as she deserved and as was the custom in similar cases; and the third being that she would not be interred in the place where other criminals were buried.

Moreover, continuing to pray to God that He pardon her for all her sins, we asked her whether she fully understood what she had been condemned for, at which she did not want to respond for some time. But, finally she declared openly that [...] God that he would pardon her [...] as well as her other sins.

Moreover, having gone a little further, she asked if one of us would take a small diamond and a little ring that she had hidden in her hair to give to one of her sisters, named Nanon, to whom they belonged. We promised that we would do so.

Moreover, having asked her about how she had obtained the poison that she used to kill the children, she responded that it was at [...] and that she had purchased it in a shop near the Fusterie market.

Moreover, having asked her how she got the children to eat this poison, she responded that, having purchased it in a granular form rather than as a powder, she had not dissolved it in either bouillon or in wine, but had soaked it in melted sugar and made it into pieces of candy.

Moreover, she had carried it to Laconnex, having mixed them with real candies that she had purchased from a neighboring merchant woman.

Moreover, having arrived at the said village of Laconnex where her child was staying, she gave some of it to her child to eat.

Moreover, having asked her how the child of the peasant woman had been poisoned and whether she had also given some [candy] to him, she responded that her intention had not been to poison him, but that he had poisoned himself because, upon seeing these candies in the hands of her own child, to whom she had given them, he snatched a piece and promptly swallowed it and it was in this manner that his poisoning had come about.

Moreover, on several occasions while speaking to her about the particulars of the said poisoning, she protested that she did not want to implicate anyone, above else she sought to absolve her cousin, who had gone with her to Laconnex, and affirmed that she alone was guilty.

Moreover, she confirmed, in general, the essence of this declaration to *Auditeur* Perdriau.

Moreover, having arrived at the foot of the platform, and hoping to give her some freedom to say her prayers to God, we told her to go up onto the platform, which she did. We followed right after her.

Moreover, once there and having kneeled in order to say her prayers out loud, after saying them and having stood up, and having been urged to speak directly to the onlookers, as she had done before, and even to make a public confession of her sin, she did one and then the other.

And first, she urged the people and particularly those of her sex [...] speeches that men made to them [...] sins of another who [...]. And next, having prayed [...] to make known to the people the public confession that she [...] of her crime, because she did not believe to have [...] to be heard, she added to the effect that [...] because this was how she thought [...] by the mouth of the pastor.

And several times she repeated that [...] truly guilty of poisoning and that she asked the forgiveness of God.

Finally she herself made this confession while speaking directly to the people, from her own mouth, roughly in these terms, "I testify to the glory of God and to my great shame that I am entirely guilty of the poisoning for which I have been condemned and that it is with justice that the council makes me suffer and be punished."

Geneva, July 27, 1686
Pinault, minister
Léger, minister

--------------------------- FOLIO 60 ---------------------------

[July 31, 1686. Deliberations of the Small Council.]

Saturday, July 31, 1686.[43] Nobles Jacques Pictet, syndic; Gallatin; de la Rive; Chabrey; Rocca; de Normandie the Younger; Lect; Franconis; Lullin the Elder; Choüet absent. Monsieur the Lieutenant present.

The man named Angevin. Jeanne Catherine Thomasset. The Lord Syndic Pan reported what happened in the prison with regards to Jeanne Catherine Thomasset. He learned from Sieur François Régis that the man named Vallotton, her relative, had admitted to him in secret that he had delivered three *écus* to the man named Angevin, guard of the prisoner, in order to convey personal notes to her and to receive some from her, upon which he instructed the Lord Lieutenant to seize him and imprison him.

--------------------------- FOLIO 61 ---------------------------

[July 31, 1686. Testimony of Pierre Seure, otherwise known as Angevin.][44]

Testimony of Pierre, son of the late Julien Seure of the city of Angers in Anjou, aged about forty-five years.

Why is he a prisoner?
He does not know.

*Has he not already testified in front of the Lords to have given some notes to
Jeanne Catherine Thomasset while he was guarding her cell?*

---

[43] AEG RC 186, F. 198.
[44] AEG procès criminels, 1e série 4704.

He appeared in council last Tuesday regarding this matter.

Did he not act as the guard of the said Thomasset?
Yes, the gaoler, Sieur Galline, came to his home and led him to Monsieur
Choüet the Elder, who made him take an oath to faithfully keep watch over
the said Thomasset.

Did he guard the said Thomasset for a long time?
He kept watch over her for ten consecutive nights, locked up with her in the
room in which Sieur Galline had put her. He was relieved at around six
or seven o'clock in the morning at which time he left the prison until the
evening in order to conduct his business in town.

*Did he, during the time that he guarded her, ever speak with a shop boy who lived
at the house of Sieur Jean Bessonnet?*
He does not remember having spoken with any shop boy who lived at the house
of the said Sieur Bessonnet.

*On which day did he speak with the relatives of the said Thomasset at the Inn of
the Golden Head?*
About three weeks or a month ago, while doing his work, a man dressed in
black with short auburn hair, who said he had some affairs to conduct with
the window-maker Sieur Chenaud, had the deponent repair one of his shoes
and invited him for a drink at the Golden Head Inn. When the deponent
went with him to the inn, they met a one-eyed man, also dressed in black,
and another fat man, who seemed to be called Monsieur the *Châtelain*.

Did he not know that these men were relatives of the said Thomasset?
He is not certain, but it is true that the said Widow Ris told him they were her
kinsmen and they declared it to him as well.

*Did these kinsmen not solicit him and did they not, in fact, give him some notes to
give to the said Thomasset?*
No. They gave him no notes at all because he advised them that he was no
longer keeping watch over her.

Did he not bring writing materials to the said Thomasset's cell?
No.

Who gave him the notes that he then gave to the said Thomasset?
Since he received nothing from anyone, he did not give her anything.

Why did he receive three or four écus from the kinsmen or friends of the said girl?
He received no money from anyone regarding this case.

*Did they not promise him handsome compensation, besides money, provided that
he give her the notes and receive her reply?*

No.

Did the said Thomasset give him a message to send back to her kinsmen or friends?
No.

Did the shop boy of the said Sieur Bessonnet or some other person not give him money and some missives to give to the said Thomasset?
No.

What did these kinsmen ask him to tell the said girl and what reply did she make?
They did not ask him to do anything once they learned that he was no longer guarding her.

Summoned to speak the truth.
Says he has done so.

Does he not acknowledge making a mistake?
No, he is not guilty of any disloyalty.
Witnessed testimony read aloud, confirmed, and signed.

Pierre Seure.
Du Puy, *auditeur*

References

Atkinson, Clarissa W. *The Oldest Vocation: Christian Motherhood in the Middle Ages*. Ithaca: Cornell University Press, 1991.

Balserak, Jon, ed. *A Companion to the Reformation in Geneva*. Leiden: Brill, forthcoming 2021.

Baudraz, Benjamin. "Les Thomasset, famille vaudoise de petit noblesse rurale (1335–1959)." *Bulletin généalogique vaudois* (2004): 112–43.

Beam, Sara. "Gender and the Prosecution of Adultery in Geneva, 1550–1700." In *Women's Criminality in Europe, 1600–1914*, edited by Manon van de Heijden, Marion Pluskota, and Sane Muurling, 91–113. Cambridge: Cambridge University Press, 2020.

— "Rites of Torture in Reformation Geneva." *Past & Present* 214, no. 7 (2012): 197–219.

— "Turning a Blind Eye: Infanticide and Missing Babies in Seventeenth-Century Geneva." *Law and History Review*, 1–22. https://doi.org/10.1017/S0738248020000218.

Brannan Lewis, Margaret. *Infanticide and Abortion in Early Modern Germany*. New York: Routledge, 2016.

Brockliss, Laurence, and Colin Jones. *The Medical World of Early Modern France*. Oxford: Clarendon Press, 1997.

Broomhall, Susan. *Women and Religion in Sixteenth-Century France*. London: Palgrave, 2006.

— "'Women's Little Secrets': Defining the Boundaries of Reproductive Knowledge in Sixteenth-Century France." *Social History of Medicine* 15, no. 1 (2002): 1–15.

Broomhall, Susan, and Stephanie Tarbin, eds. *Women, Identities and Communities in Early Modern Europe*. Aldershot, UK: Ashgate, 2008.

Broye, Christian. *Sorcellerie et superstitions à Genève (XVIe–XVIIIe siècle)*. Geneva: Le concept moderne, 1990.

Carroll, Stuart. *Blood and Violence in Early Modern France*. New York: Oxford University Press, 2006.

Chappuis, Loraine. "Enquêter, baptiser, réprimer: Le contrôle de la bâtardise à Genève au XVIIIe siècle (1750–1770)." *Crime, histoire et sociétés* 18, no. 1 (2014): 57–79.

Christopoulos, John. "Interpreting the Body in Early Modern Italy: Pregnancy, Abortion and Adulthood." *Past & Present* 223, no. 1 (May 2014): 41–75.

Clark, Michael, and Catherine Crawford, eds. *Legal Medicine in History.* Cambridge: Cambridge University Press, 1994.

Cohen, Elizabeth S. "She Said, He Said: Situated Oralities in Judicial Records from Early Modern Rome." *Journal of Early Modern History* 16, no. 4/5 (August 2012): 403–30.

Cohen, Elizabeth S., and Margaret Reeves, eds. *The Youth of Early Modern Women.* Amsterdam: Amsterdam University Press, 2018.

Cohen, Elizabeth S., and Thomas V. Cohen. "Open and Shut: The Social Meanings of the Cinquecento Roman House." *Studies in the Decorative Arts* 9, no. 1 (2001): 61–84.

Cohen, Paul. "Torture and Translation in the Multilingual Courtrooms of Early Modern France." *Renaissance Quarterly* 69, no. 3 (2016): 899–939.

Collard, Franck. *The Crime of Poison in the Middle Ages.* Translated by Deborah Nelson-Campbell. Westport, CT: Praeger, 2008.

Cowan, Alexander. "Gossip and Street Culture in Early Modern Venice." *Journal of Early Modern History* 12, no. 3/4 (2008): 313–33.

Davis, Natalie Zemon. *Fiction in the Archives: Pardon Tales and Their Tellers in Sixteenth-Century France.* Stanford: Stanford University Press, 1987.

De Renzi, Silvia. "Medical Expertise, Bodies, and the Law in Early Modern Courts." *ISIS: Journal of the History of Science in Society* 98, no. 2 (June 2007): 315–22.

Evans, Tanya. "'Unfortunate Objects': London's Unmarried Mothers in the Eighteenth Century." *Gender & History* 17, no. 1 (2005): 127–53.

Farr, James R. *Hands of Honor: Artisans and Their World in Dijon, 1550–1650.* Ithaca: Cornell University Press, 1988.

Ferraro, Joanne Marie. *Nefarious Crimes, Contested Justice: Illicit Sex and Infanticide in the Republic of Venice, 1557–1789.* Baltimore: Johns Hopkins University Press, 2008.

Flouck, François, Patrick-R. Monbaron, Marianne Studenvoll, and Danièle Tosato-Rigo, eds. *De l'ours à la cocarde: Régime bernois et révolution en pays de Vaud, 1536–1798.* Lausanne: Payot Lausanne, 1998.

Fosi, Irene. *Papal Justice: Subjects and Courts in the Papal State, 1500–1750.* Translated by Thomas V. Cohen. Washington, DC: Catholic University of America Press, 2011.

Fraher, Richard M. "Conviction According to Conscience: The Medieval Jurists' Debate Concerning Judicial Discretion and the Law of Proof." *Law and History Review* 7, no. 1 (Spring 1989): 23–88.

Froide, Amy M. *Never Married: Single Women in Early Modern England*. New York: Oxford University Press, 2005.

Gautier, Léon. *La médicine à Genève jusqu'à la fin du XVIIIe siècle*. Geneva: Jullien, 1906.

Geltner, Guy. *The Medieval Prison: A Social History*. Princeton: Princeton University Press, 2008.

Gerber, Matthew. *Bastards: Politics, Family, and Law in Early Modern France*. Oxford: Oxford University Press, 2012.

Gowing, Laura. *Common Bodies: Women, Touch, and Power in Seventeenth-Century England*. New Haven: Yale University Press, 2003.

— "Secret Births and Infanticide in Seventeenth-Century England." *Past & Present* 156, no. 1 (1997): 87–115.

Hardwick, Julie. *Sex in an Old Regime City: Young Workers and Intimacy in France, 1660–1789*. Oxford: Oxford University Press, 2020.

Harrington, Joel F. *The Faithful Executioner: Life and Death, Honor and Shame in the Turbulent Sixteenth Century*. New York: Farrar, Straus and Giroux, 2013.

— *The Unwanted Child: The Fate of Foundlings, Orphans, and Juvenile Criminals in Early Modern Germany*. Chicago: University of Chicago Press, 2009.

Heijden, Manon van der. *Women and Crime in Early Modern Holland*. Leiden: Brill, 2016.

Jackson, Mark. *New-Born Child Murder: Women, Illegitimacy and the Courts in Eighteenth-Century England*. Manchester: Manchester University Press, 1996.

Kettering, Sharon. "Strategies of Power: Favorites and Women Household Clients at Louis XIII's Court." *French Historical Studies* 33, no. 2 (Spring 2010): 177–200.

Klapisch-Zuber, Christiane. *Women, Family and Ritual in Renaissance Italy*. Translated by Lydia G. Cochrane. Chicago: University of Chicago Press, 1985.

Langbein, John H. *Prosecuting Crime in the Renaissance: England, Germany, France*. Cambridge, MA: Harvard University Press, 1974.

— *Torture and the Law of Proof: Europe and England in the Ancien Régime*. Chicago: University Chicago Press, 1977.

Lescaze, Bernard. "Crime et criminels à Genève en 1572." In *Pour une histoire qualitative: Études offerts à Sven Stelling-Michaud*, 45–71. Geneva: Presses universitaires romandes, 1975.

—, ed. *Sauver l'âme, nourrir le corps: De l'Hôpital général à l'Hospice général de Genève: 1535–1985*. Geneva: Hospice général, 1985.

Lipscomb, Suzannah. *The Voices of Nîmes: Women, Sex, and Marriage in Reformation Languedoc*. New York: Oxford University Press, 2019.

McClive, Cathy. "'Witnessing of the Hands' and Eyes: Surgeons as Medico-Legal Experts in the Claudine Rouge Affair, Lyon, 1767." *Journal for Eighteenth-Century Studies* 35, no. 4 (2012): 489–503.

McKenzie, Andrea. *Tyburn's Martyrs: Execution in England, 1675–1775*. London: Hambledon Continuum, 2007.

Merback, Mitchell. *The Thief, the Cross, and the Wheel: Pain and the Spectacle of Punishment in Medieval and Renaissance Europe*. London: Reaktion Books, 1999.

Mottu-Weber, Liliane. "'Paillardises,' 'anticipation,' et mariage de réparation à Genève au XVIIIe siècle: Le point de vue du consistoire, des pères de familles et des juristes." *Schweizerische Zeitschrift für Geschichte* 52, no. 4 (2002): 430–47.

Mottu-Weber, Liliane, Anne-Marie Piuz, and Bernard Lescaze, eds. *Vivre à Genève autour de 1600*. 2 vols. Geneva: Slatkine, 2002.

Myers, William David. *Death and a Maiden: Infanticide and the Tragical History of Grethe Schmidt*. DeKalb: Northern Illinois University Press, 2011.

Nadezda Jilek. "L'infanticide à Genève aux XVII et XVIIIe siècles (1600–1798)." Master's thesis, University of Geneva, 1978.

Naphy, William G. *Plagues, Poisons and Potions: Plague-Spreading Conspiracies in the Western Alps c. 1530–1640*. Manchester: Manchester University Press, 2002.

— "Secret Pregnancies and Presumptions of Guilt: Infanticide in Early Modern Geneva (1558–1642)." In *Politics, Gender, and Belief: The Long-Term Impact of the Reformation: Essays in Memory of Robert M. Kingdon*, edited by Amy Nelson Burnett, Kathleen M. Comerford, and Karin Maag, 265–87. Geneva: Droz, 2014.

Poncet, André-Luc. *Les châtelains et l'administration de la justice dans les mandements genevois sous l'Ancien Régime (1536–1792)*. Geneva: Presses universitaires romandes, 1973.

Porret, Michel. "La 'jeune fille mal gardée' ou le ravissement de Colette Schweppe: Anatomie d'un rapt de séduction au XVIIIe siècle." *Equinoxe*, no. 20 (1998): 57–68.

— *Le crime et ses circonstances: De l'esprit de l'arbitraire au siècle des lumières selon les réquisitoires des procureurs généraux de Genève*. Geneva: Droz, 1995.

— "Limiter l'arbitraire du juge dans la qualification du crime: L'enjeu des pratiques médico-légales à Genève au XVIIIe siècle." *Clio Medica* 31 (1995): 187–204.

Pullan, Brian S. *Tolerance, Regulation and Rescue: Dishonoured Women and Abandoned Children in Italy, 1300–1800*. Manchester: Manchester University Press, 2016.

Rieder, Philip. "Miracles and Heretics: Protestants and Catholic Healing Practices in and around Geneva 1530–1750." *Social History of Medicine* 23, no. 2 (2010): 227–43.

Roth-Lochner, Barbara. *Messieurs de la justice et leur greffe*. Geneva: Société d'histoire et d'archéologie de Genève, 1992.

Rublack, Ulinka. *The Crimes of Women in Early Modern Germany*. Oxford: Clarendon Press, 1999.

— "Pregnancy, Childbirth and the Female Body in Early Modern Germany." *Past & Present* 150, no. 1 (1996): 84–110.

Soman, Alfred. "The Anatomy of an Infanticide Trial: The Case of Marie-Jeanne Bartonnet (1742)." In *Changing Identities in Early Modern France*, edited by Michael Wolfe, 248–72. Durham: Duke University Press, 1997.

Sperling, Jutta Gisela, ed. *Medieval and Renaissance Lactations: Images, Rhetorics, Practices. Women and Gender in the Early Modern World*. New York: Routledge, 2013.

Spierling, Karen E. "Making Use of God's Remedies: Negotiating the Material Care of Children in Reformation Geneva." *Sixteenth Century Journal* 36, no. 3 (2005): 785–807.

Sussman, George D. *Selling Mothers' Milk: The Wet-Nursing Business in France, 1715–1914*. Urbana: University of Illinois Press, 1982.

Terpstra, Nicholas. *Abandoned Children of the Italian Renaissance: Orphan Care in Florence and Bologna*. Baltimore: Johns Hopkins University Press, 2005.

— *The Art of Executing Well: Rituals of Execution in Renaissance Italy*. Kirksville, MO: Truman State University Press, 2008.

Trabichet, Anne-Sophie. "'Tant que l'on nourrit, l'on rit?' Être nourrice à Genève au XVIe siècle." Master's thesis, University of Geneva, 2018.

Tuttle, Leslie. *Conceiving the Old Regime: Pronatalism and the Politics of Reproduction in Early Modern France*. New York: Oxford University Press, 2010.

Vermeesch, Griet. "Facing Illegitimate Motherhood in Eighteenth-Century Antwerp: How Changing Contexts Influenced the Experiences of Single Mothers." *Continuity and Change* 34, no. 1 (2019): 117–37.

Warner, Lyndan. *Stepfamilies in Europe 1400–1800*. New York: Routledge, 2017.

Watt, Jeffrey. *The Consistory and Social Discipline in Calvin's Geneva*. Rochester: University of Rochester Press, 2020.

Witte, John, and Robert M. Kingdon. *Sex, Marriage, and Family in John Calvin's Geneva: Religion, Marriage, and Family*. Grand Rapids, MI: W.B. Eerdmans, 2005.

Index

J.C. stands for Jeanne Catherine Thomasset. Page numbers in italics represent illustrations/maps/sample documents.

Printed and bound by CPI Group (UK) Ltd, Croydon, CR0 4YY

13/04/2025

14656517-0005